WEATHERING

Poems and Recollections

David Havird

MERCER UNIVERSITY PRESS
Macon, Georgia
2020

MUP/ P600

© 2020 by Mercer University Press
Published by Mercer University Press
1501 Mercer University Drive
Macon, Georgia 31207
All rights reserved

9 8 7 6 5 4 3 2 1

Books published by Mercer University Press are printed on acid-free paper that meets the requirements of the American National Standard for Information Sciences—Permanence of Paper for Printed Library Materials.

Printed and bound in the United States.

This book is set in Adobe Garamond Pro.

Cover/jacket design by Burt&Burt.

ISBN   978-0-88146-734-5
Cataloging-in-Publication Data is available from the Library of Congress

CONTENTS

ONE

TWO

THREE

FOUR
RECOLLECTIONS

FIVE
EARLY POEMS

...with age
Feeling more in two worlds than one   *in all worlds the growing*
    encounters.
    —James Dickey, "The Shark's Parlor"

ONE

PHALANX

I watch it, this turtle, and picture
a tombstone that stood here, a sculpted hoplite
wearing a conical helmet and hugging his shield,
and think is crawling that hoplite,
his blood now colder than marble. Yes,

like the falling and budding of leaves,
the lives of hoplites and turtles. In that museum
displaying the hoplite charging, another one
stationed itself at my ankle inside the café
and stretched out its neck and begged.

They have no vocal cords, but can,
retracting their heads when startled, hiss.
This one, I thought, unless I let a flake
of pastry spotted with spinach fall—this one,
its neck a kettle's spout, will spit and scald.

They're everywhere, an epic transmigration
of echoes, ghosts of the myths' one turtle
scooped from its shell by Hermes,
a cattle-rustling, wing-heeled toddler,
who strung the shell with cow-gut—eureka!

the lyre, whose wandering pulse,
which formed an ode, since lost,
to one Aristonautes the hoplite, bears
a shield amid dull spears of grass
and soldiers on, an urn among red poppies.

WEATHER ON NAXOS

The god, his humors petrified as veins
in roughhewn marble, was going down
feet first from the quarry, down to the port
where there is now a whitewashed village—from there
to the other side of the sea,

which moves in front of the tables,
the wobbly blue and white taverna,
only enough to glisten. I climbed
until I had the whole of him at my feet.
I had as well as a wedge of spinach pie

a plastic half-liter of Naxian red.
It came to me to stream a swallow down
on that colossal archaic rockhead,
effaced though he had been by wind and rain—
as also sprang to mind this god

as a fidgety infant snug in the crook of an arm,
his older brother jangling grapes
to disenthrall the spirited boy
from who knows what is making him fuss, while I'd
inspirit a lull, would rouse the weather

inveined in coolheaded marble. Up
the mountainside, the flight of slippery
marble slabs, into the quarry
schoolchildren surged, to scramble up
the unfinished god, to scurry over him,

between the stubs of reaching arms to plop,
from bearded chin to feet (a pedestal
this column never stood on, much less danced
as Dionysus) to heel-walk slide—
a revel of wind and rain in the vineyards.

DOWNHILL FROM THE MARBLE VILLAGE

I went by public bus to the marble village,
Saturday's end of the line.
Square slabs of marble paved the thoroughfare;
steep marble steps climbed to the upper levels.
Marble the archways that gave on a cavernous
maze of mule tracks, marble paved.

A sign near the bus stop directed me to a church.
How long it would take to walk there and back who knew?
The grassy pathway down was sometimes steep,
with jagged rocks, which pointed upward, and thistles,
not to mention the plastic bottles,
cellophane wrappers, wads of white tissue.

My sandals, right for the port, for my loitering there,
were wrong for the hike downhill from the marble escarpment.
Their rubber foot beds gripped the soles of my feet,
gripped them with sweat like glue—
it was, without much shade, a blistering trek—
while step by step inertia tested the bond
and every roll of an ankle ruptured the grip.

Early Byzantine, the church
belonged to the seventh century, maybe the ninth—
left open page-down on my bed, the guidebook knew—
and boasted if not a kissed-bleary icon,
maybe some fresco fragrant with soot,
worth a squint if luck found a door unlocked.

The way was not for sandals—I turned back—
much less for shoes, or so the bells,
as I translate their summons, tell;
but rather for feet, bones bruised, soles pierced and bleeding,
the pilgrim's bare feet. I should, they're tolling, the bells
of the portside cathedral this Sunday morning at seven—

I should have kicked those goddamned sandals off.
The site attained and myself shed of my lading,
from that deep vein I'd have as good as winged
my way uphill? Sheer agony
it would have been returning feather-heeled,
bedazzling though the destination was
and cool because it was marble.

SUBWAYFARER

They laid him out and settled upon him
Athens after Athens. Below the square,
three thousand years ago deep,
a bone arm lifts—I saw it, radius
and ulna. In truth

it was the arm of a subwayfarer's reflection,
a see-through tourist in transit
whose hand with its camera palms whatever it eyes,
the man in the wall forbearing, his glassed-in skeleton
holding the pose.

CROWN OF THORNS

A tree up from our broken reality...Keeping faith.
—Rolf Jacobsen (trans. Roger Greenwald)

When we got down, there ambled toward us
a large white dog with a blue bandana
in place of a collar, and one of the children
had to stoop and *ooh*, her face
in its one only face, and it—

it wagged its tail. But once we'd assembled,
toed the length of the platform, its master,
bleached-blond Mohawk, bomber jacket,
combat boots with red laces, and something
whisky-brown in an Evian bottle, *oohed*,
his face in ours. He snarled, while back and forth,

flinging his middle finger up,
he strutted, paused..."Don't even glance his way,"
I breathed to Trina, whose eyes were tearing.
That gesture, did he have it right?
he asked in English. A chorus of nods,

that one child mouthing *oui*. He spat
viciously onto the tracks, then off he marched
to an exit, the white dog trotting behind him.
Our stop was Trocadéro, the summit's view
of the Eiffel Tower sparkling. Later,
after we had toured the Catacombs,

we pictured the Métro as shelf on shelf
of skulls. Down there, I told the children,
I'd heard again as through the broken grin
of skulls Coach Pinkerton snarling, "You think"
(we boys who huddled on wooden benches),

"you're all so young" (in our fresh uniforms),
"you're going to live forever, but me,
I know I'm not. Every morning
the coach in the mirror whispers *You
are going to die*" (each of us huddling more deeply
into himself), down where stone dark can't tell

if finger bones or roots have seized it, roots
"planted in our humiliation," up
from which a tree burgeons over the earth,
its crown amid the stars. So down we went,
and there was a dog, if only a one-headed mutt

whose master it was that bared his teeth and snarled,
blond Mohawk, red-laced boots, who flipped us off.
Then up, as though we scaled that tree,
to skitter along a lamplit street
as though along a shimmering branch,
the skyline prickling with thorns of light.

VANISHING POINT

Hendrick Cornelisz. van der Vliet,
Intérieur de l'Oude Kerk à Delft *(1660–1670)*

Already (my birthday, falling in mid-October,
a week away) pumpkins on stoops
and witches with brooms and gauzy spooks
asway on wrought-iron railings. These
disturb the grid that is at dusk
our habit to walk, a grid of blocks—

galleries, one and then another
until a church in Delft, the floor of its nave,
siphons my vision. Flanked by colonnades,
arcades with pointed arches,
beneath a wooden vault: a stone-slab grid—
receding lines that aim as though at God

as through the eye of a needle,
the rood screen's doorway into the shadowy chancel.
Stone slabs, some few of which a man,
waist-deep in the floor,
whose red shirt draws the eye away—
this man's pried up and swiveled aside.

Around him in heaps—
his right arm propped on the shovel,
against a column the broom—
a graveful of dirt. Waist-deep in the grave,
he's hearing out a white-collared elder in black
with a Puritan hat on. Loose dirt and clods,

with bones, which look like clods, mixed in. A grid
of square stone slabs, converging lines that find,
I see, in the dusk of the chancel
the red-shirted grave's new body…She bristles,
the dog does. A long, low growl
inches me up on whatever is new to sniff.

BECOMING SAGE

We went for a drive, those two old men and I.
I drove, and Milo, whose car it was, rode shotgun.
Earle, in back, wrinkled his nose
in the rearview mirror. "That smell—what is it?" Drove west,
the river, glinting with sunlight, running beside us,
the redwoods lunging sunward out of view,
and then—so steep were the cliffs
and such a long way down it was to the shoreline
whose rocks the ocean kept pawing with foam
even while swimming sleekly, if not
forever outward, all the way to the sky—
south along the coast and inland. "Mice gnawed
through the wiring," Milo said of his vintage T-Bird,
which shared the garage with this car. "Must be
a mouse." "In here, you mean"—Earle shifted
his weight—"somewhere in here there's a carcass?"

We lean, my host and I, on his wooden railing.
"Last night, did you hear it—the wildcat?"
So that's what it was! Lying awake in the dark,
I pictured from schooldays a planetarium's dome
of heavenly bodies, the night sky whole
as I, a city boy, had never seen it,
while to my ears they seemed, those planets and stars
(among which there were some that weren't there now,
were tributaries only, sourceless streams
of milky light), to clot and drown in globs
of rain, through which somehow a sharp
scream like a probe had stabbed me awake.
"The Mexicans," Milo remarks, "were scheduled to start
at 2 a.m." I watched them yesterday early
creeping with plastic tubs along the rows

13

of vines—how they'd each grab a purple bunch
and slice it off with a short, curved blade. "Too wet
today. No rain, though." Milo gestures: "See
the silver linings?" The clouds—they're gray;
where puffy, white. "Maybe," I say. He squints
at me. Testing me is he? "Can you," he says.

Tonight we charcoal steaks (today was my birthday),
uncork a years-old red from when our host
made wine. He sniffs it, wrinkles his nose and tastes,
pokes out his bottom lip and shakes his head.
"Wine is a living thing, and this Merlot—
either it was getting really good,
like nothing the two of you have ever drunk,
or else it was going bad." I quaff it. We toast
with one of his Syrahs. The night sky's back
to spilling milky light from many points.
That river's running. I drift as though downriver.
Earle and I, when driving in,
had to brake for a wolf. The dashboard clock
told midnight and there on our left in moonlight lay
the asylum. "Look," I said. "An inmate's escaping."
Milo scoffed when told. "A prairie wolf
you mean." In one of those tipsy cuplike boats
I drift, becoming sage or not. It scampered
under our high beams, a werewolf. "We'll start tomorrow,
the Mexicans will, on the Cabernets. Small grapes,"
Milo observes, "they yield less juice,
but the flavor is more complex."

HURRICANE-PROOF

That rasp—the ceiling fan?
Or rats? At night rats climb the palms,
the manager said. Don't sleep
with the doors to the balcony open. Besides,

sea wind's salt; everything metal
it rusts. She rapped the glass—
Paloma-proof!…The AC whooshes on.
In your mind's eye Paloma's heap,

twisted siding, splintered boards,
ragged sheetrock, glass-toothed muntins—fix
though you would that eye
on birds (blue sky, white loops of flight),

white baton tails
and narrow blades of black-tipped wings
and orange beaks (strain though you do
to train your ear on their reedy chirps),

beside the limestone bluff whose seams
they jet into and nest within—
that season's rental
bulldozed off, the concrete slab

scraped clean…Or hold in view
(the AC cycling off, that rasp!)
the morning's yellow-crowned night heron
toeing on yellow marsh-reed legs

the lip of the pool and piercingly
eying—*there*, it stabs, beaks up,
with that black beak which spears
the crabs that cloister themselves

in a salvage of shells
from the locals' harvest of sea snails,
a gurgling throatful of water—
red hermits amassing at sundown

under the fronds where you, the two of you…
It was as though the sunset,
while it impassioned you and this other
snoring beside you, whose sleep is

hurricane-proof,
hemorrhaged claws, a tide
that armored itself in spiral shells
for its incursion inland.

MINING FOR SKY

1.

The Schuman twins were digging to China,
so here was the neighborhood in their back yard.
We kids were all of maybe four feet tall—
down there were they six feet under?
I picture only roots as their way out.
Some grown-up quipped, "What's this—
our first bomb shelter?" The Russians were coming.
No one pictured boiling up from the sky,
clambering up those roots a column of Red
Chinese. A first for the neighborhood,
the hub of that square wheel of starter homes.
Even before we kids left grammar school,
everyone moved: the Fulmers next door on Beltline,
the Robinsons over on Craig,
the Schumans on Oakview—Oakview,
where I rode bikes with the Robinson boys.
The parents now, like mine: one foot if not both in the grave.
There's no escaping the pit. The bomb shelter either.
What was it but a tomb stocked with such staples
as lined a grandmother's pantry?
Stocked for the long descent past roots to sky.
But there they are—I rarely played with them;
those boys were mean, the Schuman twins—
mean how, I cannot remember—Tommy and Timmy,
blond bangs, their heads emerging.

2.

From hereabouts the Swamp Fox bushwhacked the redcoats,
and hereabouts in the brush was a holding cell
for the captives, now a mere depression filled
with leaf-mulch. We're walking through woods,
my wife and I along with her brother
whose home is here on the farm where they grew up—
through woods where legend also places a graveyard.
Not even their grandfather ever heard tell of the markers.
They must have been wooden. Stepping through mire
and talking "green burial." Steve,
though he believes—he really does believe—
in something "over opposite, against,"
has warmed to the topic. "Say," I ask,
"do you ever see any foxes?" Crossing the pasture,
we noticed the tracks of white-tailed deer,
the plats of their furry scat,
observed the ravaged ground of rutting boars.
He's never down here at night,
but sometimes, up at the house, he's seen one,
a gray fox up from the swamp attacking the pawpaws.
In thought I'm mining for sky. I've read, you see,
about a Chinese spirit, a scarlet fox,
a minx of low cunning whom age makes grandmotherly wise—
home-wrecking vixen, celestial fox.
"That's it, a pawpaw!" I say,
the kind of tree I want my body to nourish.
I've pictured myself, a modest bone-framed home
in root-trellised earth. Day is breaking
below me. A fox, exquisite barbarian, brush
glistening faintly with moonlight, creeps
through the sunrise. The wild bananas above me
have softened. The ripeness of nightfall guides the red fox
to the calcified sun in my bones.

TWO

THE BASIS OF SOMETHING

When I was a boy, we had a maid named Carolyn.
Or was it Caroline? There's no one to ask.
Carolyn *Who*? I wouldn't have known.
How old I was I don't remember either—
only that we lived in the house on Beltline
and I was…how old when we moved from there?
It doesn't matter. I was a child; she was
our maid. She looked like…How did I know
what Eleanor Roosevelt looked like? I went
with my parents to see *Sunrise at Campobello*.
But there it was Greer Garson. Besides,
what stayed with me was what she sounded like.
"Fraank-*lin*!" she hollers, right as the movie opens.
The theater laughed. She sounded just like her,
Mother later explained; Greer Garson had down pat
Eleanor Roosevelt's "head voice." (A musical term—
would my mother have used it?) However—
maybe I'd seen her picture in *World Book*—
I did know what she looked like, and Carolyn,
lanky, long-boned and horsey-faced,
with crinkly, graying hair pulled back in a bun,
looked like a colored Eleanor Roosevelt.
She was my days. My mother had too soon
gone back to teaching. Whenever Carolyn ironed,
I'd ask her, if she didn't tune to it first on her own,
to find us the colored station. The radio sat
on the bedside table, next to my father's side
of the bed—next to my mother's, her desk and chair.
(A window unit made my parents' bedroom
the only air-conditioned room in the house.)
I loved…what was it—gospel? Rhythm and blues?
She'd fix me lunch, a hotdog sliced lengthwise

and fried (boiled when my mother had fixed it)—fried
it must have been in the bacon grease
Mother saved in an aluminum
stovetop canister. After her lunch,
she'd smoke in the kitchen, a Pall Mall, which she shook
from a red pack. Pall Mall was a "quality" brand.
I see her running a finger along it.
She's pointing something out, which has to do
with how the edges adhere. You couldn't see—
I thought she meant the seam, plain to see
though it was. The glue? What wasn't I not seeing?
Riding the bus from wherever she lived,
she brought me one of those tiny, aquatic turtles,
red-eared with yellow-striped green head—
I'd maybe cajoled her after first begging my mother—
from one of the downtown five-and-tens,
Woolworth's, Kress's, McCrory's.
I'm wanting to make it a symbol, to see
that dime-store turtle if not as a cosmic
world-bearing turtle, at least as the basis of something...
Carolyn even wiped me. *Caroline*—
is that the name I'd holler out when done
(though capable more or less myself)
and she'd unroll, hand over hand, a ball
of tissue and give my fanny a quick once-over?...
Something or other's foundation. What I see
is the turtle floating dead in the fishbowl,
the water's dingy surface speckled with food,
like flakes of tobacco, when we got back
from being gone. One day, Carolyn
didn't show up. Nor did she the next day, nor
the next. For that was how they quit on you.

THIN DISGUISE

The ferry was bobbing and creaking.
Head bobbing, I pictured the rocker at home,
also my mother as she must have pictured herself
when she and her sisters were sorting Grandmother's things:
a new mother there at her mother's
rocking her colicky boy. Why else had she wanted it,
oak with a drab upholstered seat and back?
Its creaking put me to sleep,
she shrugged, as nothing else could.

I slept my first night through on the island,
on sea-legs staggered to breakfast, a lavish affair
conjured up by a witch in black leggings.
Was it the apron or was she acquiring a paunch,
this Circe, behind whom sauntered
in place of a panther a calico cat?
Sleeveless her black knit top. On her bronze arms
I fixed the ravenous gaze of a wayfaring man.

At dinner I hog an outdoor table for four.
I slide the knife along the spine of my fish
while eying a couple who've swayed downhill
as if they strayed from a revel. She's wooing,
this blonde with short shorts on
and a blouse that slips from a shoulder
or rises to show her navel whenever she motions,
out from between the menu boards
maybe the calico's kitten,
while her young man, gripping with one hand
a bottle of wine by the neck, picks at his whiskers,
the tourist's first beard, with his other, and what I feel
on my new face, a breeze

from the harbor, where my beard was
is like cold fingertips, the sinking sun's, which read
as through a thick disguise a bald-faced lie;
and when the sun, despite its lens of cloud,
finds on my leathery wrist,
right as I lift with the blade white flakes of meat,
white hairs amid the brown like feathery fish bones,
I picture in place of her feverish boy
a graybeard without any beeswax to stopper his ears,
a bone-heaped beach in place of the lap of his mother.

THE SPELL

Ακολουθει

I picture you with a knife
in one hand, the sandal
upside down in the other,

wanting a third
to angle a mirror.
Follow me

your footprints spell
in the dust. Amid the rubble
on either side

of the Street of Tombs,
not a stele standing. Where
have you swished off to, cruised

through what gate's leer
(I've come ashore
with harpoon eyes),

toxic white
with mulberry lips,
swinging your hips like a fishtail?

NATURE MORTE

A laurel wreath of gold encircling his head,
Napoleon holds aloft a bejeweled crown
for her, for Josephine, who kneels
three shallow steps below him. We who know
scarcely a living soul in the gallery know
who they are, that pair in matching regalia
(crimson velvet busy with golden bees
and ermine-plush) and snap salutes
with our smartphones. Those others who dwarf us?
A card on the wall depicts them in outline,
each of them boasting a number that goes to a name
on a list. If only one could worm his way
through this too solid throng…though who among us
will not swear in a foreign tongue that he's melting?

You turn, and she, whose name you read,
Madame Récamier reclines on a sofa.
White muslin tumbling from her crossed ankles lures
the eye to her feet, while the see-through sleeve invites…
Her stare defies you to run your gaze
along that bare forearm to those bare feet.
A black hair band…*restrains* you say to yourself
as though the curls were writhing. Nesting rather. Sets
them off—as does this other's red
hair ribbon. Red too the sash around her waist.
White sleeveless gown (a peplos, yes?) baring a shoulder,
Élisabeth-Louise Vigée-Le Brun
enfolds in long, white arms her nine-year-old
Julie, whose arms, in blue short sleeves,
encircle her mother's bare, white neck.
Faces with names that turn your way, whose stares
you return—you aim your phone. Each time I do,

she's there, an older woman,
her brown hair yielding to gray at the temples—one
my age. All right, whoever you are
in your black skinny jeans, white poet blouse,
I'll snap you too. A glance my way, a nod,
and off she scoots. At whatever paint-fixed face
I aim because its look has caught her eye,
at whatever face with a name, away she shies.

A distant gallery offers lunch
on a shiny salver, a herring, which eyes me, a roll
on the wooden table, Rhine wine
in a tall, thin flute (and an earthenware pitcher).
Now there's a snack with ham, rolls too
and…are they bagels? and sliced brown bread,
a wheel of yellow cheese and one of white,
the carved cold joint in a clove-studded jacket of fat
arranged on a wooden table, on creased
white linen, from which a knife extends
to me its pewter handle. After all,
how could I not be hungry? I'm hungry for real.

IN PLACE PIGALLE WITH MY FATHER

I pose across from the Moulin Rouge. "Red mill,"
says one of the guys I'm with who aims, then phones me
home to my wife. We're having dinner
farther up in Montmartre, and when I see me,
after the waiter has poured us wine,
a grassy Sancerre *blanc* that's new to me
as I am newly French in Gatsby cap
and scarf, I grin as there I don't:
across from the music hall, iconic windmill,
its sails a wheel of light, I'm Parson Solemn.
I'd gone in my mind, you see, in search of my father.
It's early morning; he's traveled overnight
alone by bus from wherever in Germany Ed,
his nephew, is stationed. Not since World War Two
has he traveled abroad and only now, nine months
a widower, to Europe. On his bald head
a cap not unlike mine except it's tweed,
and owl-eyed frames upon his big nose perched.
She seats herself beside him, a makeup-bruised
coquette; and he—"*Il n'y à pas de quoi*"—
mouths out the only French that comes to mind.
"*Il n'y à pas*"—throws up his hands—"*de quoi!*"
That bench—could it have been in Place Pigalle?
In thought I sidled through the milling throng;
amid the grassy median again,
I failed to spot it. Him I did sight, past
the breakers, the two of us together, treading
water, and there he sported a red...no, garnet
gamecock-emblazoned baseball cap
while telling about some widow—"Berley,"
she said ("Imagine," my mother sometimes teased,
embracing him, kissing his shiny pate—

"imagine naming a tiny baby *Berley*"),
"they'll claim, a lot of women my age will,
that they don't like it, but me—I like to screw."
He grinned, and came those dimples. I envied him
his charm, a man who "never met a stranger,"
who later confessed that when it came to sex,
"I wasn't ever strong"—he'd had as a teen
a "severe case of the mumps"—and brought to mind
the scene in which my wife and I tell why
there isn't a grandchild yet for him and my mother.
Says he in that chest-out tone of his, "I thought
you maybe were impotent—mumps," and winks.
I'd gone, I had, in search of my father
who told in mime with widower's hands how my mother
had fastened his palm to her belly—I pictured a wife
beginning to show who guides her husband's hand,
my old man's freckled hand and hers blue-veined,
over the swelling—or he'd have never found
how full it was and firm with something wrong.

LES MOUCHES

After the cloudburst I follow the gravel path
to the garden. A concrete wall to my right
deflects the snarls of traffic. Thin woods to my left,
its leafy branches shading the path. From these
an occasional raindrop, one of them staining my sleeve.
Right as the cat-piss odor of boxwoods bites,
I spy through the trees a backside, black like mud.
The path then doglegs left, and there's a woman
whom I must dodge. Now viewing Eve straight-on—
this black bronze Eve that lowers her head
and with one arm hiding her breasts raises the other,
hand to face palm outward, forefeeling the blow—
I picture the woman, a trim brunette
in slim black slacks, whose sallow complexion
was horribly pocked…as if the blow struck her
instead. The blow? A look that scars.

As Rodin's Eve looks like black mud or tar,
there was about her features
an earth-emergent look, a clayeyness,
that makes me at first forget: Adam only it was
for whom God modeled clay; for Eve, carved bone.
Soon, however, I have in my mind
a bone-white Eve, like a marble antiquity,
whose perfectly oval face with chiseled features,
catching a look that puts her down,
grows lumpy, sallows, shading to russet—becomes
if not exactly clay to be kneaded and pinched,
something of earth: an apple, yes, of earth
with eyes like scars that bud and probe the dark.

I turn from Eve and have to squint.
The after-shower suffusion of sunlight hurts,
and there's a thrilling scent, which piques the mind
with a fragrance from childhood: the zest
in clothes that dried in the sun.
Even after every house in the neighborhood, ours
included, boasted a dryer, my mother preferred
to hang the washing on backyard clotheslines—and did so
until new next-door neighbors with bird dogs laid
a concrete slab and erected a hurricane fence,
and up at the property line goes a kennel
breeding flies that speckle
the pillow cases and sheets,
those otherwise radiant whites
that billow, flap and snap,
rummaging high and low for wings.

WEDDING WIND

Beyond the pines, which hid, except for the chimney,
a closed-off-season beachside taverna,
from up on the slope where, relics ourselves,
we lodged in a derelict windmill,
the blue looked firm enough to float a rock

without a ripple of worry. Even so,
my gaze, as though white-robed, a savior,
skimmed to the boat in the cove,
then stepped from the solid blue of the bay
to shelves of bluer schist, a pilgrim,

on up to the whitewashed church on its finger of rock
to exchange with the icon a kiss
for a healing look from the Virgin. Wind
by evening. We took our sunset walk
around the wind-chopped cove,

the sailboat-pitching cove,
along the cliffside path
despite not only the wind but also the crowd
thronging the church. A wedding, yes.
Among the dusty cars that choked the lot

was one in a wind-whipped frenzy
of streamers. The spirit aroused, of course, in us
a vision of ours. By ten, electric guitars
were yowling. The pines—were they dancing with wind
or light from the woken taverna? The wind

swelled with the odor of meat fat sizzling on coals;
the taverna was smoking. Or wasn't it thunder
that shook us, that fiendish, vibrating bass,
and cats, the feral ones fed by our landlord
to battle the vipers, serpents of lightning?

In bed as though on board,
we drowsily hoisted a sail
too suddenly pregnant with wind—our rope-burned hands
like urgent semaphores, like creaking blades
up on the slope conducting the wind.

UPON THIS ROCK

Two days of it, wind from Africa
shoving the sea from its bed. The Sahara
erased the horizon, hazed the islands
from view. But now across a bay as blue
as it is calm, as blue as the churches are white,
on the tip of each of two narrow peninsulas
gleamingly white—across the shimmering bay
a fishing boat putters. Over my shoulder
a dove coos; farther inland the bells
of the blue-domed basilica toll.
Call and response. When next from down below,
from somewhere amid the stand of pines
between this place and the shoreline,
a rooster crows, I go in my mind,
I shoulder my way—head down,
again I am butting my way through the wind
to the edge of the cliff: wind-steepened waves
a crown, and wind-torn wisps like tatting,
the sea a god's bulk bursting against the face
of the cliff, the depths like batting
up through a hole in a boulder
exploding. Hearing the rooster, I picture the rock
hawking the sea from its throat;
I think of the fisherman Peter
erupting with curses, in agony crowing.

SHOOING FLIES

I found the car key.
Maybe I ought to have sped to the port.
Thanks to a taxi, you were there
even ahead of time awaiting the ferry.

Instead, I braved the switchbacks,
narrow, gear-strippingly steep,
up that treeless rock
whose peak is St. Simeon's perch.

I pictured you, umbrellaed, gazing the harbor.
Lean out from under the shade and shoot your gaze
up to the blue-domed church.
Is somebody up there waving?

I meant to distance myself
as far as I could from the port of return,
spirit from body. Away, though,
hadn't we relished our bodies!

Out in the bay where a fisherman
netted an icon depicting the Virgin,
beside her whitewashed church
on the severed tip of a finger of stone

I'd fished for you with my eyes,
then handled ashore love's shivering body,
which ached for another, the friction,
to redden its blue-lipped flame.

Who would have dreamed there'd be above it all
a nimbus of flies! Somebody, yes,
was waving and, bitten as if by sparks,
shooing flies.

THREE

MOLTING

Before dawn even, zipping past the exit
to Myrtle Beach…That's where my girlfriend was
who had a summer job there singing.
But I was heading north
to see Janet. Hot and muggy, the weather
changed at Richmond to rainy,
not with a torrent of blades but a drizzle of pins,
and chilly. I had to borrow a flannel shirt
from Janet—a man's, which fit me. Janet was renting,
along with her college roommate
and one other girl, a townhouse in Georgetown.
Sometimes, while they were at work,
I'd venture afield to a gallery,
Corcoran, Phillips; mostly I browsed
the neighborhood bookstores and otherwise loitered.
I had to ask the girls, because I was getting
so many probing looks from guys,
if maybe I had an effeminate manner.
"You have," she said, the matronly one whose name
escapes me, "just a nice face." I slept
on the living-room sofa. Sunburned, itching like mad,
I'd scroll the peeling skin off my shoulders
and roll it into a little ball,
then flick it. Overhead, the women
were getting ready for bed, their heels
conveying thunder while I read by lamplight
a poem in *Harper's* by Robert Penn Warren,
whom Janet and I and her housemate Felicia had met:
"A Problem in Spatial Composition,"
in which a hawk, like something divine,
unseen above a window-framed vista
composed of a stone scarp and forest,

39

at sunset enters the frame as if from forever
only to go "in an eyeblink." My wife,
who was then my girlfriend, who sang at the beach
where noontide had blistered my shoulders—
my wife says it's all about sex. Not Warren's poem,
this story of mine. The thunder, having slung
flimsy bras across the shower rod,
puts up its feet—the women, nesting. Molting,
I clasp the neck of that shirt, whoever's it is,
which I'll shake out in the morning.
The weather whistles past windowsills
and under the door, and though it sings
like blades' cold steel, I picture
within the lamplight's moon on the ceiling
a hawk whose shrills are high noon's killing rays.

THE WEIGHT OF A FEATHER

We waited at sundown,
swamp chill adhering to soles,
for ducks to show
(stragglers they looked to be, the three or four)
in the strip of sky between the snarl of treetops.

"Sure was a fine shot by one of you boys"—
a party of hunters trudging by us,
and Dan and Scott, small boys
but hunters for real already, laughing,
pointing at me, the city boy

whose shotgun wasn't his,
nor did he have a license
nor waders on for the swamp
where beavers lodged and the alligator that ate them
nor dog along to retrieve it—my one duck ever.

Reading a poem, "Mallard," by R. T. Smith,
who must be a hunter also for real—
the make of his gun? Wingmaster.
Mine? Search me—
I envied that hunter whose memory finds

a satin drake in the mouth of his hound,
sheen dimming while still in its eyes
the sunrise bleeds on the river,
who "shivers" to think of his heart's load judged
"against the weight of a feather,"

41

as you can see it done in the Book of the Dead
by a bird-beaked god with a balance,
behind him poised the crocodile-headed Devourer.
More than my share of ducks, which Dan and Scott
pluck and gut in the sink in the mudroom,

have I devoured—breasts marinated in what
it is their secret, bacon-wrapped
and charcoal-grilled.
More than my just portion?
I gorge to find the one in one bite more.

PRAYERS FOR A GIANT

For Anthony Hecht

My mother, a girl then, was sitting on their verandah,
facing away, when a cat smacked down on her back,
locking its claws. A boy, whose only pleasure
was meanness, had sneaked around the magnolia
and pitched it. That incident preys on me, hunched at the wheel,
our daughter in back with nothing—
not even a naked giant, scored in chalk
on the hillside, wielding a wide-toothed club
and boasting a huge erection—
to make her forget she's starving.
(Remember, it's your pilgrimage, not hers.)

"Here," in Stinsford churchyard, "lies the heart
of Thomas Hardy." *When day of Judgement be come,*
Almighty, 'e'll say, 'Ere be 'eart
but where be rest of 'e? "Westminster Abbey,
Poet's Corner—remember the tablet?"
The story goes—we sit on the gravestone,
Rachel and I, amid the shade of a yew—
that when they came for the heart, they found the tin
in which the surgeon had laid it, this cookie tin
on its side, top off, the tea towel lining it
out, and Cobweb licking his bib.

Tonight her prayers include a petition
not for the smoke-colored Persian, interred in the churchyard
while still the heart's fresh grave, but for Midnight,
drowned on her grandparents' farm before she was born,
whom Rachel remembers because of one story:
still a kitten, Midnight mewed at the door

43

and when let in made us the gift of a bunny.
With green eyes looks at us, looks down at it,
she paws it, peers at us...
It went straightway, a fist-tight wad,
into the garbage can outside.

A star's reflection plunging, the well's heart thumps.
The giant tugs loose from the grass and plants himself
in the sky—*Lift up your hearts. We lift them up
unto the Lord*, whose white breath swallows
even the spires of London. I wake up numb—
I've bedded down, it seems, in my own ashes.
The comforter over me now,
my heart again declaims by rote its prayer
that its last beat may be a new star's first.
Breathing out a trumpet of fog,
I feel throughout my frame pulsations of starlight.

HAUNTING THE SHROPSHIRE WAY

Sometimes the footpath became a hollow way
through a coppice. Then it was like an aisle in a church,
minus the gravestones. *When they lie flat,*
they're meant to be walked on—these invite
our feet to talk with the dead. Shoes off,
I planted myself on a slab
that told of Jane Austen, but not
a whisper tickled my roots.
Then Housman's stone, cedar-garlanded, sat
outside, where I could only pose
at wrought-iron bars, and anyway
grass softens the chatter of feet.

An aisle? I hopscotched through mud as though through one
long grave. The rout of lads
who beat the footpath down where now roots scratched
my ears—their fleetness of foot
showed in their absence. At fifty,
I knew myself to be faring
with my own lightfoot ghost.

The footpath, crossing a pasture, arrived at a stile.
A farm road angled. One leg, trampled to mire,
met the carriageway somewhere uphill.
The footpath merged with the other:
along one side, barbed wire, the soil below it
cascading; across from this,
a stone retaining wall. Between:
a sluggish river of dung. I stepped
down from the stile into slurry. On tiptoes

I forded that Styx, then hoisted myself with elbows
over the wall, shouldering bushes aside.
Awake, I cannot picture the manor—
whose rose-lipt daughter was where? A lamb
sporting in evergreen shade
with what lion? I kept to the footpath
in spirit, trespassing, yes,
but tripping along the wandering edge of the garden,
whose fragrant shrubs screened off
the soggy pasture, the slough.

No sooner did my feet reclaim the way
than spatters began to blacken my parka, rain
like spit. But then it drenched the stubborn grass
besieging the footpath, tussocks
inviting my feet to wipe their shoes.

SPARROW

The sparrows of Paris are the sparrows of home.
—Adapted from Randall Jarrell

I went on my sixtieth birthday
to see the parrots with Rilke
as though I too were a witness for whom they were waiting.

Fenced in of course, exotic even in Paris,
birdbrains holding in view
an immutable rainforest home,

blue-and-yellow macaws, a roosting pair
on the skeletal limb of an uprooted trunk,
tweezed each other's lice,

while down on the ground a single Buffon's macaw,
green with blue-edged wings, red brow,
teased a gooey fruit stone. Went

with Rilke, yes, but there,
above the screams, a cockatoo's,
its black tail-feathers a fan of flames, heard Yeats

crowing that he had "pretty plumage once,"
who boasted at sixty a shock of white, a crown
to be envied...What parrot's this?

The card in English reads "clown of the mountains,"
and there, but not inside the cage,
within a square of mesh, the fence his throne,

gray breast, brown wings, has perched
a sparrow—no, the one house sparrow god
who's everywhere escaping notice, there

as though to capture my eye,
as soon as done to launch himself. I dodge
it seems not quickly enough and flinch, a wing

or else the winged-through air, its cutting edge,
swiping my cheek and earlobe. Marked
for exile home, I thin to gray, homebound

among that one house sparrow's host
of avatars while you observe
or not from what blind roost, clown of the mountains?

FLÂNEUR

Auguste Rodin, L'homme qui marche *(1877–1878)*

This marble torso—even without a head
it looks at you, as though a lamp,
one of those old-fashioned gas lamps,
whispered within it, the flame turned low
even where once was that jet of procreation.

You try by looking hard to hear what it sighed
to Rilke. But come two guys,
one of whom clicks while his buddy poses behind it,
stubbly head above marmoreal shoulders,
and there appears, as though that low

flame murmured a spell, the washboard stomach,
flattop butch-waxed: that older cousin
who'd pin you down, digging his knees in your pecs...
Now *this*—a walking bronze one that looks for the world
as though a vandal whacked it or crosswinds bit

or tremors laid it low while new
and newer works of hand amassed,
a torso, which that marble one, the flare
of its gaze, discerned—a find that has to tense
its abs to keep from wobbling atop the stride

and stressing those sutures of solder—atop
what massive legs, which cast their look on yours,
and you have wrestled off the plump duvet
to lie revealed, a fleshy torso pale
as marble, and all of a sudden, the cramp

seizing a calf, you find your legs,
feet too—how they do ache,
pressing the cold parquet. They redden
as though from within, this bronze
pedestrian's legs, a foundry of muscles simmering.

THE FOX AT ANCIENT ASINI

Those bits of terracotta are pottery shards.
Some of them even display a trace
of geometrical design. And here's
the cove below that spot, blue now
which had been green, on what had been
the shaded side of the citadel. There on that ledge
when we were peering down at the cove—was it
a fox? Fox it became when it uncurled.

Now this, encircled by weeds,
is the hewn stone mouth of maybe a cistern.
The poet Seferis, when he was here with his wife,
disturbed a bat. Losing its hold,
it came at the sunlight. A spear at a shield.
Maybe the King of Asini's gibbering ghost.

In Homer's catalogue of ships,
to which Asini contributes,
the King is nameless. This absence
provokes in Seferis such nostalgia
he's able to touch the stones where *he* touched them—
where maybe he did, the points of contact
regardless abraded by time—
and trace there a palpable presence.

Whether those rocks, that limestone,
ever belonged to the castle,
the Swedes who dug here would know. I'm posing
right on the edge of the spur. Posing
as if I own it. Tolo is there—
those white hotels and tavernas lining the shore.
And that on the island's a chapel—the roof, terracotta.

My gaze embraced the bay
while I returned in thought to the cistern.
As I imagined things, its depth,
escaping the reach of our flashlight,
adhered to our soles; and our shadows,
repulsed by the shield-bearing sun,
deepened a shade underfoot.
I pictured off the coast of our home state
the crude oil billowing up
through deepwater's ruptured horizon, tar
capturing even this bay.

The purple thistles, which we had to dodge,
were leaning to snag the westering sun.
The zeal of bees in the lavender blossoms
gave the heat the scent of thyme.
We've now retraced our steps, and here we are—
or rather here's our table under a cedar:
horiátiki, yes, Greek salad,
eggplant imam, giant beans,
a sweating carafe of young white wine from Nemea.
"I glanced away, then back and found it gone,"
I say of the fox.
The red fox that awoke in the yellow weeds.

WITH BYRON AT BANDELIER

Bandelier National Monument, New Mexico

I walked with Byron the trails at Bandelier.
Out of a petroglyph
he spiraled, Odysseus
up from the whirlpool—Lord Byron

whose steps I'd followed in in Greece
in the same trail-runners.
Leave only tracks. Where native feet
had worn down narrow trails in the tuff,

which you can keep to
only with always the same one foot
in front of the other, at Bandelier
I tracked up trails

with Byron's footprints.
Take only pictures. I focused in
on one of the cliffside spirals. Whirlpool, no—
a rising sun

through whose all-seeing noon
amid charred pinyon pines
and ashen junipers, I viewed
The flying Mede, his shaftless broken bow;

The fiery Greek, his red pursuing spear
amid sheer bluffs, gaunt pines and junipers,
and slopes of olive trees like crones,
wrought-iron Fates

with silver knives, and Byron
under a whetstone sun
carving his name
as if among these petroglyphs

in marble. Noontide swirled
from the spiral. I steadied myself
against a pine and scanned
the rock face. A stick man hoisted

a stalk of maize. The Greek
with his red spear spun nightward.
The tree, though charred,
bristled as if on guard with green.

FOUR

RECOLLECTIONS

IN AND OUT OF CLASS
WITH JAMES DICKEY

Lelia's Court is a steeply descending cul-de-sac that doglegs to the left so that several lots, including James Dickey's, back onto Lake Katharine, a man-made lake beyond which lies Fort Jackson. It was the drumming from this Army base "every / Sun-up, neighbor," that so discomforted the Dickeys, Jim and Maxine and their two boys, when they settled in Columbia, South Carolina, in 1969: as the embattled suburbanite puts it in "Drums Where I Live," "now and then I wish I had a chance / To take my chances / With silence." And when Lake Katharine was drained in the early 1970s (or so Dickey told me), the vista comprised "A hundred acres of canceled water come down / To death-mud shaking / Its one pool." Surveying this expanse, the poet in "Remnant Water" can only "wait and make the sound surrounding NO." Dickey's house is a late '60s, L-shaped, ranch-style affair, a garage in front making the foot of the L.

The secretary, a middle-aged woman with blond hair, cracks open the front door. Has Dickey neglected to tell her of our appointment? Twice he postponed my visit. "I've never known you to be so inaccessible—at least to me," I finally said, and he promptly set a time for us to meet: today at noon. Out of sight of the doorway, he orders her to let me in. A ledge extending leftward from the slate-floored foyer connects the book-shelf-lined living room with the family room, and there sits Jim, surrounded by waist-high stacks of books, a tomb under construction.

What I notice first, besides the gauntness of his once round face, are the clear plastic tubes in his nostrils: "I didn't know you were on oxygen," I say before we've even shaken hands. These tubes branch off a very long one connected to a vacuum-cleaner-size oxygen-generating machine on the floor between the two rooms. "I don't really have to have it," he says and with a flourish pulls the tubes from his nose. His red knit shirt has "Kinko's" spelled out across the left breast. His

57

shanks—he's wearing shorts—are all scaly skin and shin-bone. The brown plastic-rimmed glasses loom on his narrow face. His smile reveals that one of his long front teeth has reddened....As I'm leaving and he's signing a book for the archives at Centenary College of Louisiana (where I teach), I stand at his elbow and notice amid a pervasive odor of oily, unwashed flesh that it would be possible now, in early summer 1996, to number each gray plug of transplanted hair on his head.

My father had died in the summer of 1995; now I was in Columbia, where I grew up, to dispose of his personal effects—I had sold the condominium he purchased after my mother's death in 1984. "There's no reason for me to come back," I've told Jim. Since my graduation from the University of South Carolina in 1976, I would at least telephone him whenever I visited my family. "Yes, there is," he insisted.

When I was twenty, I'd left a party there on Lelia's Court—the occasion, a visit by Robert Penn Warren—with this line of Dickey's repeating itself in my mind: "I have just come down from my father." So begins and ends "The Hospital Window," in which a son receives from his dying father an empowering benediction when the old man waves from his hospital window. But driving away from Dickey's house (which was to be sold after the poet's death in 1997 and bulldozed down to make space for a less dated house), with the burden still of clearing out my father's clothes from his seventeenth-floor condominium, I felt as if I had stepped into the role of the son in a similar, autobiographical poem by Warren: "After Night Flight Son Reaches Bedside of Already Unconscious Father, Whose Right Hand Lifts in a Spasmodic Gesture, as Though Trying to Make Contact: 1955." That gesture, because of its ambiguity, blackens, "snatch[es]" from the son "all things," his unrealized aspirations as well as his triumphs.

When I was fourteen and in the ninth grade, Dickey delivered the commencement address at the University of South Carolina. My father, a graduate of the Law School (as well as the College of Liberal Arts), took me to hear the poet. It was my father's custom to attend the commencements; he had no special feeling for poetry, boast though he did of winning a bet with a co-worker who insisted that there was to be "no mourning at the bar" when Tennyson "put out to sea." "No moaning, moaning," my father would repeat, "no moaning of the bar."

On June 1, 1968, I'd never heard of James Dickey, but he had already published his *Poems 1957–1967*, the retrospective selection upon which his critical reputation still mainly rests. (*Deliverance* appeared in 1970.) He was now completing two terms as the consultant in poetry at the Library of Congress; he was to join the English faculty at the university in 1969.

In those days the spring commencement took place on the red-brick Horseshoe, the original site of the university, which curved past the president's house, old dormitories, and the South Caroliniana Library. The Horseshoe encompassed a shady lawn, and it was here that a temporary platform stood, in front of which were rows of folding chairs. "I'll bet he's not much of a speaker," my father predicted when Dickey, a charismatic public performer, rose to the podium.

Afterward I was eager to meet the poet. In contrast to my father, who stood at only five feet, eight or nine inches, the black-gowned Dickey, at six-three, epitomized "body-authority." Always one for promoting his kid, my father bragged that I could "dash off" poems. "That's something I can't do"—Dickey was shaking his head. In *Self-Interviews* Dickey says, "I look with absolute amazement at the work of poets who just do two or three drafts and then, brother, there it is!... If I had a pretty good poem on the third draft, I would think, 'Boy, this is going to be really good when I have really worked on it!'" Real poets didn't just toss off poems. Even so, the poet autographed my program, "To David Havird in the community of letters—James Dickey."

However grudging I may be to claim my father's alma mater as my own, it was at the University of South Carolina that I studied under James Dickey and met such poets as Allen Tate, Robert Penn Warren, Robert Lowell, Richard Eberhart, and Archibald MacLeish. Stephen Spender, whom I met when he lectured there on Auden, writes in *World within World* of his Oxford days: "During this early period of my meetings with the Great, I experienced those agonies of longing for their friendship which can hardly be explained to those who do not understand what it is for a young man to start trembling when he recognizes in a crowd the face of someone who means to him, Poet." My father, who'd later speak of my "rebellion," was expecting me to become a lawyer like himself. Now I seemed to need if not the friendship of the Great, the blessing of a poet of my father's generation.

A month into my second year at the university, on September 28, 1972, I'm sitting in Dickey's office, across the desk from him, while he peruses some poems of mine: "'The prodigious sun'—perfectly beautiful, I think." But he must "live with these awhile." Meanwhile, why don't I join him later at Lum's, after his classes?

Within walking distance of the university, Lum's is famous for its hot dogs steamed in beer. Pabst bock is on tap there, and Dickey and I each order an ice-glazed mug. I have with me the Vintage paperback of John Crowe Ransom's *Poems and Essays*. Dickey taps its black and pink and yellow cover. "You know," he says, referring to the Fugitives, "the one of them that I like best of all is Robert Penn Warren." The source of Warren's appeal is his "passion" and "force"—and scatological imagery: "There's as much shit in Warren as there is in Swift."

Dickey's remarks later as well as then composed a variation on this passage from *Self-Interviews*: Warren, he observes, "is a desperate, ghoulish, nightmarish kind of writer with a very Swiftian strain of excremental and other repulsive imagery. Warren's hysteria and violence are as powerful as anything in American literature, and I like that immensely." And yet there was another Warren, as Dickey sees him in a review of *Being Here: Poetry 1977–1980*, "starry-blooded, a night-walker, a night-watcher, a searcher lying motionless," whom Dickey came to regard as maybe "the best Warren of all." At Maxine's funeral in 1976, Jim himself read the lovely, visionary conclusion of Warren's *Audubon*: "Tell me a story....Make it a story of great distances, and starlight." Warren might have been the only living American poet whom Dickey never trashed.

At Dickey's invitation I begin sitting in on his graduate-level seminar in modern poetry. Its fall semester is devoted to American poetry. Dickey enters the room. Putting down his attaché case, he abruptly shouts: "'We want Daniel, Daniel, Daniel'—let's hear it, three times!" I understand later that Vachel Lindsay and his poem "Daniel"—he of the lions' den—figured in Dickey's previous lecture. Here Lindsay's lions clamor for the prophet.

Though Dickey frequently ad-libbed, a large, three-ringed, black binder, with typed-out lectures, always lay open on a desk, behind which he sat—except on one occasion when he placed the chair on top of the desk and, with the aid of his female graduate assistant, mounted the throne. These lectures (since edited, some of them, as *Classes on Modern Poetry and the Art of Poetry* by Dickey's colleague Donald J. Greiner) included a biographical sketch and Dickey's own incisive critical generalizations, which he then illustrated by first setting the scene and then reading aloud a representative poem. Never did his presentation of a poem include a "Brooks and Warren" analysis; he'd typically pause after this or that line and remark with wonder, "Isn't that good!" Forty years later I am still hearing Dickey's "performance" of specific poems then new to me: "Hurt Hawks" (Robinson Jeffers), "Say Goodbye to Big Daddy" and "Burning the Letters" (Randall Jarrell), "The Vow" (Anthony Hecht).

At Lum's, Dickey slaps down a five-dollar bill, which more than covers the tab. A wide-brimmed black felt hat on his head, he drives away in a sapphire-blue Jaguar XKE, its ragtop down. Later, in 1976, while drunk and en route to a trysting place, he will wrap this sports car around a telephone pole.

In the early '70s Dickey, who liked big hats, seemed to favor a black felt hat with a four-inch brim and pinched crown, stuck in whose band was a turquoise, white, and red feather.

"Say, Mister, I love the way you wear that hat"—I am remembering a line from the movie *Deliverance* that Bobby speaks to the hillbilly pumping gas. We're waiting for an elevator in the lobby of the humanities classroom building. Dickey squints down at me. I'm expecting the hillbilly's contemptuous reply, "You don't know nothing"; instead, he removes the hat from his head and holds it upside down so that I can read the small, silver lettering on the sweatband: *The Shadow*. Dickey intones, "Who knows what evil lurks in the hearts of men?"

There was about Dickey a demonic or, better, a Dionysian aura; it had the scent of alcohol and sometimes garlic. As Dickey's drunken alter ego in *The Zodiac* insists, "Whiskey helps. / But it does. It does"—fuels, that is, the creative act. During my first year at the university, *Deliverance*—the movie—appeared; one wondered at the perverted psyche that had dreamed it up. Of course we guys in moments of tom-foolery would grab one another's ears: "Squeal like a pig…wee, wee!" One similarly wondered at the demented brain that had given birth to such poems as "The Sheep Child" (spoken in part by a "woolly baby / Pickled in alcohol," the product of sexual congress between a Georgia "farm boy" and a sheep) and "The Fiend" (whose third-person narrator depicts empathetically the night life of a homicidal peeping Tom, "a worried accountant," outside an apartment complex). It was easy for the adolescent mind with at best a scant knowledge of literature not to see that such poems, self-consciously allusive as they were, had endured a long gestation within a literary, even scholarly intellect. Dickey em-bodied the allure of forbidden knowledge. We were emboldened by his authority to descend into those shadowy, profane settings within our own unconscious psyches. There we would discover our divinity. Whether its character was fiendishly bestial or Messianic, it did not matter. We had no doubt that we would not merely survive the katab-asis but emerge intensified. It remained for the wakeful, inventive poet-as-craftsman to channel that volatile "night life" into a form that con-served its force, such as the three-beat anapestic line, the "night-rhythm," of Dickey's own sober, formal, early stanzas.

Dickey's authority depended not only on his authentic genius but also on the theatrical figure that he cut—a sometimes melodramatic figure that strained for effect, courting absurdity, daring ridicule. Still, you had the suspicion that Dickey also saw that this figure was some-times ludicrous, but what the hell? Someone told me—but how could he have known?—that Dickey, on a hunting trip, had killed with a bow and arrow a rabbit whose blood he then smeared on his face. No hunter myself, I did know from Faulkner's *Go Down, Moses* that this ritual followed your killing of your first deer. In that novel young Ike

McCaslin, under the tutelage of Sam Fathers, kills his first buck, and this archetypal Wise Old Man dyes the boy's face with the sacrificial blood. The story about Dickey and his rabbit became entangled in my mind with this and a later hunting episode in *Go Down, Moses,* and the result was a poem, "Ike McCaslin: An Epilogue." Here, in a moment of self-delusion the old Ike of Faulkner's "Delta Autumn" becomes again young Isaac "by Sam Fathers' side" and downs his prey, only to discover while smearing his face with its blood that he has killed not a deer but a rabbit.

"We're going with that one," Dickey announces. (During the early '70s Dickey was the poetry editor for *Esquire*; he was accepting "Ike McCaslin: An Epilogue" for publication there.) It's November 1973, a Sunday evening, and I'm standing with some friends at a party we students are hosting for Robert Penn Warren and his wife, Eleanor Clark. They've spent the weekend with the Dickeys at Litchfield Plantation, a complex of condominiums on the South Carolina coast. Just returned, Dickey's wearing a blue-jean jacket, the back of which is emblazoned with an American eagle holding in its claws a banner that reads not "Liberty" but "Poetry"—that "one word, raggedly blazing with extinction," as Dickey depicts it in one of his "False Youth" poems.

Warren is in Columbia to receive the University of South Carolina Award for Distinction in Literature, the brainchild of James Mann, a graduate student in English (more recently the poet of *Tombstone Confidential*), and Professor George Garrett. (The award honored Allen Tate in the spring of '73. Lowell will follow Warren as its recipient in April of '74.)

Warren arrived at the airport, incognito as it were, sporting a Vandyke. As he remembered in a letter twelve years later, "I had a sort of white beard left over from our canoe trip into the upper Canadian wilds. The trip to Columbia made me cut it right off. You guys would courteously seize my elbows to get me across the street or up the stairs. Great God, you were rushing me into my grave. Or into a wheelchair." I'd walked him down the hill from Capstone House, a women's dorm boasting hotel-style guest accommodations, to the apartment on Green Street where several of us students were giving the party in the

Warrens' honor. The roots of huge trees that occupied the space between sidewalk and street had caused the concrete to buckle; and given that it was dusk and that Warren could see out of one eye only, it seemed prudent to steer him around or over the upheavals. He jerked his elbow from my grip.

When Jim Mann and I, having fetched the Warrens at the airport, got them to the Dickeys' on Friday, Dickey was just stepping out of the shower, and so the four of us chatted with Maxine in the foyer. When he did emerge from his toilet, he went straight for Warren, ignoring Jim and me. I studied Dickey, his swept-over mat of brown hair still wet from the shower, but stiff with spray—looked hard at him, hoping in vain that my stare would draw from him at least an acknowledgment of my presence.

On Friday, then, I might as well have been invisible as there in Dickey's house with Robert Penn Warren. Understandably perhaps. But despite the beer at Lum's—much less that inscription from the 1968 commencement—I'd never had a name; I'd always been "my boy." Now it's only two days later, Sunday, and at our party for the Warrens Dickey is announcing his acceptance of "Ike McCaslin" for *Esquire*....It never appeared there. Had Dickey's acceptance of the poem been a charade or was his designation as Poetry Editor a sham? I never dared to ask.

The Dickeys themselves host a party after Warren's Monday-night reading. An elderly, white-jacketed black man tends bar in the family room; Maxine has made guacamole and hot clam dip. Most of the guests are English professors. Some of us, including Warren, are sitting there, Dickey and I together on a sofa, Warren at a right angle to us in a black leather-and-steel director's chair. Dickey seizes from the glass-topped coffee table a volume of his own—we've hearkened, so the gesture says, to Warren long enough—he opens it and proceeds to introduce "Under Buzzards." The poem carries a dedication to Warren, and Dickey identifies him as the "companion" who accompanies the speaker, Dickey himself, into the piney woods of North Georgia. "Do I have to go?" Warren's face crinkles with mischief. Dickey snaps, "You're going, my man!"

"Under Buzzards," in *The Eye-Beaters, Blood, Victory, Madness, Buckhead, and Mercy*, is one of a pair of poems whose collective title is "Diabetes." Dickey has never had diabetes, has never taken insulin, as does the speaker of "Diabetes." But here he is in "heavy summer" on Hogback Ridge; buzzards, the "birds of death," are circling, sensing as they do the lethal sugar in his blood. Should he inject himself with insulin and so maintain a healthy balance in his blood—between too little sugar and too much? Affirm life as a middle way? Or should he embrace glory, first by crushing the syringe with a rock and then demanding that his companion "open that beer"? That gesture—an ad-man-turned-poet's endorsement of the Miller High Life. But then Warren in *Brother to Dragons* also affirms that "drink's a kind of glory..., though sleazy."

Other guests have gathered around us. Maxine's mother, Mrs. Tipton, is standing behind me, leaning against the sofa, one haunch resting on the back, and swaying. Dickey's introducing another poem, "Blood." It's about "screwing—you've been screwing, and you're drunk; you wake up, and there's blood all over the sheets, the room, and you think, My God, has someone been murdered—because, you know, you're drunk, you've been passed out; but then you realize, because you've been screwing, that she's having her period, and it's not the blood of death but the blood of life—the blood of life." The emotion in Dickey's voice ranges from shouted desperation at the beginning of the poem—"mercy, MERCY!"—to cloying tenderness at the end, when the speaker, ignorant of the woman's identity, insists that it's of "no matter," for "she is safe" (portentous pause): "She is safe [pause] with me." In fact, she is safe with him because his "weapon"—that is to say, his phallus—"will never recover its blood": the episode has rendered him impotent. Dickey later told me that the incident behind the poem took place at Allen Tate's house; I didn't believe him.

Abruptly Dickey turns to me: "David"—which he pronounces *Devid*—"I want you to hear a new version of 'Dueling Banjos.'" He stands; I stand, ready to follow. "Anyone else," he says off-handedly, "is welcome." A number of us, not including Warren, follow Dickey out of the family room and down the hall to his study. Dickey sits me down at his desk, which faces a window that looks out in the daytime

65

on the back yard and Lake Katharine. Several guitar cases lie on the floor, along with various bows; a photo on the wall boasts the autographs of three Apollo astronauts. Dickey manipulates a large reel-to-reel at my feet. We listen to some impressive flat-picking whose tune, to my ear, bears no resemblance to that one from *Deliverance*. Dickey, a faint, tense smile on his lips, is scrutinizing me, assuring himself that I'm receptive to what I'm hearing.

This invitation had really been mine alone; the other guests had been insufficiently alert to this fact, or else they had not had the courtesy to decline it. I had acquired a name. "I have just come down from my father"—for a long time afterward, this line from "The Hospital Window" ran, a refrain, in my mind.

I was then, in 1974, the editor of the student literary magazine, and in honor of Warren's visit to the university, the staff dedicated to him the fall issue of *The Crucible*. In it there was a poem of mine, and Warren observed, "It is a poem—looks like one, feels like one, tastes like one. Must be." This encouragement emboldened me to send him others, whose jerky rhythm and tortuous syntax looked for their model to the two sonnets, "Sirocco" and "Gull's Cry," that open *Promises*, Warren's Pulitzer Prize-winning 1957 collection. "You are booming along," he wrote in March of 1974. "What impresses me, at first look anyway, is the subtlety of rhythm and the way you play off complicated syntax in a stanza form...I do feel that you are the real thing. Most I feel this because the poet behind these poems feels bigger than the poems." He typically added, "Any others handy?"

After three of my poems appeared in *Poetry* in 1976, Warren generously observed, "You have certainly come far in fluency and the feel of poetic texture. Real poetry." But he cautioned,

> If I had to say something on the critical side, I'd say that I'm not
> sure that your allusiveness always works for me, now and then,
> some defect in continuity, perhaps even lack of contact (perhaps
> my fault) with a basic idea....I'm not pulling for an 18th-century
> prose mind you—but I do think the author ought to be able to give
> a good reason for the way things are in his poem. Not a bad

question to ask oneself. You might say the same thing back to me about certain poems of my own, and certainly I'm not maintaining that "logical progression" is the key to poetic structure. But I'd say that it is an element.

What encouraged me was that his qualified praise, because it was ambivalent—even the negative criticism, because it was itself generous—seemed to testify to his sincerity when he added on another occasion, "You are bound, my hunch is, to make it just fine."

During those formative years when I was a student of Dickey's, I was writing as much for Warren's approval as for his. And yet with Warren as my guide I missed the exalted sense of mission that I felt when Dickey shadowed me. In that poem of Warren's with its ungainly, journalistic précis of a title ("After Night Flight..."), the father's "spasmodic gesture," that eclipsing failure of recognition that comes with death, condemns the son to a repetition of the old man's failures. In contrast to Warren's role as son of Adam, Dickey's persona in "The Hospital Window" becomes, thanks to his father's benediction, the resurrection and the life.

No, it wasn't Warren's poems that I wanted to have written. Nor really even Dickey's. Of the Great whom I met in my adolescence, Robert Lowell was the one whose poems, as soon as I discovered them, made me burn to meet the poet. To their relentless beat, their defiant enjambments, my response was kinesthetic, visceral. I had felt my muscles flex as soon as I cracked open for the first time *Lord Weary's Castle* and read in the stacks,

> There was rebellion, father, when the mock
> French windows slammed and you hove backward, rammed
> Into your heirlooms, screens, a glass-cased clock,
> The highboy quaking to its toes. You damned
> My arm that cast your house upon your head
> And broke the chimney flintlock on your skull.

I concealed from Dickey my passion for Lowell. Presciently so. On the eve of the older poet's visit to the university in April of 1974,

Dickey was referring to Lowell as "my oldest friend [portentous pause] and rival."

Lowell was bemused: "I only met Jim a few years ago," he observed when I reported to him that characterization. The coltishness of Dickey's sense of competition revealed itself during Lowell's daytime visit with Dickey on Lelia's Court. Maxine suggested to the three of us students who had accompanied Lowell that we give the two poets time to themselves—they were strolling toward the dock. There, at Dickey's initiative, they both removed their shirts. Dickey boasted the superior physique. Lowell's skin was very pale and slack—"and he's supposed to be so attractive to women?" Maxine was incredulous. Lowell was wearing bedroom slippers—as Auden did, Maxine explained. After a while, we students joined them on the dock. Jim Mann and I sat flanking Dickey on a wooden bench. Lowell, in brown corduroy Levis, sprawled on his side on the planks of the dock, a red chamois cloth shirt and an incongruous blue suit jacket folded beneath his bare torso. Our friend Janet Lee snapped pictures. As I began to read aloud one of the fourteen-liners from *For Lizzie and Harriet*, Lowell murmured, "That's not how I would read it."

"Cal," Dickey said emphatically, "will you let the boy read?"

I am to introduce Lowell at his reading and present him with the university's Award for Distinction in Literature. Dickey approaches me in the lobby of the auditorium: he's wanting to say a few words beforehand—"to bring," as he explains, "the people to their feet." The moment arrives; he's stressing how privileged we are: hearing Lowell is "like hearing [portentous pause] Milton [pause] read." Honored it may be, but the audience sits on its hands. Dickey pleads, "I want you all to stand; will you do that for me, please?" We obey.

Lowell's plan is to begin with poems by others, all of them Southerners: "Aeneas at Washington" (Tate), "Next Day" (Jarrell), "Original Sin" (Warren), "Adultery" (Dickey). I have lent him *The Norton Anthology of Modern Poetry* (1973), which includes the poems by Tate and Jarrell. He introduces them, then stoops to retrieve the book from his briefcase. Now his domed head, with its tousle of whitening hair, oily strands of which have been sticking out ever since he removed the beribboned medal from around his neck, is emerging from behind the podium: "A nightmare thing has happened," he mutters. "I left the anthology in the motel room." ("Funniest thing I ever saw at a reading"—Dickey laughed about it on many occasions, mimicking Lowell's weirdly Southern murmur: "'A nightmayer thing has happened.'") No Tate and no Jarrell. But in his briefcase there are copies lent to him of Warren's *Selected Poems New and Old* and Dickey's *Poems 1957–1967*. It is important, Lowell maintains before reading Dickey's "Adultery," for a poet to have a good "prose style"; arranged in eleven, three-line stanzas, this poem's free verse, Lowell implies, exemplifies that commendable quality. Here a male speaker addresses his female lover during an assignation in a motel room: "Although we come together, / Nothing will come of us"; yet, the speaker insists, "Guilt is magical."

After the reading, Lowell observes that Dickey, "really a very intelligent man," disparaged him in some forum as a "slick" confessional poet—how curious the comparison with Milton! I nod, say nothing.... Dickey, who sneers on film at Milton, was stoking Lowell's vanity. In *Notebook* (selections from which Dickey has read aloud in class) Lowell recalls "calming my hot nerves and enflaming my mind's / nomad quicksilver by saying *Lycidas*" right before assaulting his father. "The Quaker Graveyard in Nantucket" is Lowell's bid for Milton's mantle.

"I think you're right," the letter from Howard Moss begins. "The influence of Lowell is felt in these poems. But something else is, too." During the winter recess I traveled to New York with a music professor and a group of students. Beforehand Dickey casually advised, "You ought to look up my editor." Moss I knew from the selection of his poems in Hall, Pack, and Simpson's *New Poets of England and America*, a text in Dickey's graduate course on modern poetry. I had by heart "Father, whom I murdered every night but one, / That one, when your death murdered me." I dialed the number for a Howard Moss in the Manhattan telephone directory. The right Moss answered and in the course of conversation cordially observed that he was now at home— yes, I knew that—but if I'd call him in the morning at "the office," we could meet during his lunch hour. He gave me the number. The office, as I discovered when I placed the call, was *The New Yorker*; I had assumed that Moss was an editor at Doubleday, which had published *Self-Interviews, The Eye-Beaters,* and *Sorties.*

A fay, bald-headed man in black plastic frames, Moss is eating a sandwich at his desk. Rollie McKenna's photographs of *The Modern Poets* decorate one wall, the one to Moss's right, of the small, drab office. "I used to ask Lowell, whenever I'd see him, to send us something," Moss says between bites, "but he never did." As I'm preparing to leave, he asks me if I write poems. I mumble that I'm trying to. "Have you ever considered sending them to *The New Yorker*?"…Yes, he's serious; address the submission to him personally, since he has a reader. In the letter that soon accompanies my submission, I defensively acknowledge the "Lowell hand."

Dated January 28, 1975, the letter from Moss has just arrived. "I'll be in *The New Yorker* by the end of the year," I boast to Dickey on Groundhog Day. It's his birthday, February 2; he's wearing his presents from Maxine, burnt orange double-knit slacks and a white, cable-knit sweater. With my friend, Ashley Mace, whose family owns a cottage at nearby Murrells Inlet, I'm spending the morning with the Dickeys at Litchfield Plantation. He narrows his eyes. The laugh—is it skepticism, ridicule? Or the wordless, vocal equivalent of the go-for-it slap on the back? Surely the latter.

In fact, I was then writing the poem, "End of a Year," that Moss accepted in early March. It tells about some wasps—two dozen by my count—that swarmed into my bedroom in October through a "cleft wood awning." In the course of the poem, which moves from fall to winter, all that remains of this "grim platoon" of wasps is a straggle of camp followers (the speaker's "old lovers"), while the troops themselves, like the ranks of the pharaoh, advance on Bethlehem. It had intrigued me to learn in a seminar on Colonial American literature with Calhoun Winton that South Carolina was on the same latitude as the Holy Land. In Lowell's "Where the Rainbow Ends," "the scythers, Time and Death, / Helmed locusts, move upon the tree of breath." So my wasps compose an orbiting nimbus around the head of the infant Christ. Though Moss apparently found the "Lowell hand" less evident in this poem than in the earlier ones, my poem's oracular concluding lines echoed the last stanza of "Near the Ocean." (Much revised, and minus the last four lines, "End of a Year" appears as "Wasps in Winter" in my 2013 collection, *Map Home*, and with an additional change in *Weathering*.)

"Is it a short poem?" Dickey asks. Hardly anyone else has yet arrived for class. "Well," I reply, "it's fifty lines." Dickey's eyebrows rise....If he ever read this "long" poem, as he then described it, which had met with the approval of his editor, he did so in *The New Yorker* where it appeared in November.

Having got the bachelor's degree in the middle of the academic year, I am, in the spring of 1975, a first-semester MA candidate, now formally enrolled in the second semester of Dickey's course on modern poetry. But I've been hearing from Ashley Mace about the submissions to his *Seminar in Verse Composition* from the mysterious Silver Skin. The fall semester of this two-course sequence focused on form: the epigrammatic couplet, the quatrain, the sonnet—villanelles and sestinas awaited the ambitious students. The spring semester stresses revision. For the first assignment the student submits two prose narratives—of a dream and a masturbation fantasy—and a free association. Dickey then chooses for each student the most inventive one of these—the one that most seems to promise a poem. The process of revision, which begins with the isolation of evocative diction and arresting images, then commences. This spring, contributions have been arriving from a student unable to attend the workshop, fragments signed "SS," for Silver Skin. The pseudonym, as Dickey has explained, bespeaks the disfiguration that afflicts this non-traditional student thanks to his years of working a South American silver mine.

Dickey has himself been detaching phrases from obscure poems, ranging from a sonnet by Frederick Goddard Tuckerman to stanzas, which rather sound like Dickey's anapests, by a contemporary Australian poet unknown to American readers. At the end of the term, these phrases will appear in the finished poems.

Having asked to see me after class, Dickey is now proposing that I appear as Silver Skin on the last day of the workshop; he'll then expose the ruse. He will supply a costume. That afternoon, we arrive at the classroom ahead of everyone else; he shuts the door, withdraws the get-up from a grocery sack. When the students do enter, there I am, crouching, head down, hugging my knees, in a corner—on my feet a huge pair of huaraches; a purple fringed suede jacket hangs from my shoulders, covers tent-like my bent legs; on my head that wide-brimmed black hat whose sweatband spells out *The Shadow*. When I raise my head, I'm holding, pressing against my face, a silver life mask of Dickey himself. With only one hand free, I struggle to my feet before I take it off.

SOUTHERN RELATIONS:
WITH ROBERT LOWELL
AT TIMROD'S GRAVE

In April 1974 Robert Lowell read at the University of South Carolina. This wasn't Lowell's first visit to the state in April. In 1947, according to Paul Mariani, "At Easter...he was in Charleston, South Carolina, 'admiring the old houses,' and visiting Fort Sumter, 'horrified by the flat, coastal desert that surrounds it'" (Mariani, in *Lost Puritan: A Life of Robert Lowell*, quotes from the poet's letter to his aunt Sarah Winslow). It was, of course, the Rebel bombardment of Fort Sumter in April 1861 that started the Civil War, and it was the Union assault on Fort Wagner, on nearby Morris Island, in 1863 by a "bell-cheeked Negro infantry" led by Colonel Robert Gould Shaw (whose sister married a Lowell) that Lowell commemorates in "For the Union Dead."

If "St. Gaudens' shaking Civil War relief," the bronze monument depicting Colonel Shaw and the African American Fifty-fourth Massachusetts Infantry, links Boston Common to Charleston harbor, perhaps (or so Mariani implies) the "[p]arking spaces," which "luxuriate like...sandpiles in the heart of Boston," brought to Lowell's mind the sandy spit where Fort Wagner stood and "half the regiment," after the unsuccessful assault, lay dead—to be interred in a mass grave, a "ditch," by the victorious Confederates. According to the historian Thomas J. Brown, at least some of the Confederate casualties repose in Charleston's Magnolia Cemetery, the decoration of whose graves, among other Confederate veterans' graves, in 1866 occasioned an "Ode" by Henry Timrod, the unofficial poet laureate of the Confederacy. Lowell's visit to South Carolina in 1974 culminated in a pilgrimage to Timrod's grave in a churchyard in downtown Columbia across the street from the Capitol.

If you want to picture Lowell as he looked while on that pilgrimage, find in Ian Hamilton's 1982 biography of the poet the 1974 photo of Lowell with his almost shoulder-length, scraggly gray hair—he's wearing a dark suit and a knit tie with horizontal stripes. You can't see on his feet the Clarks sand suede Wallabees, which amused my mother, who mistakenly recognized them as Hushpuppies. In her judgment these would have gone all right with the red chamois cloth shirt and baggy brown cords that Lowell had on at James Dickey's house the previous morning, but not with a suit, much less a dark blue suit. Then, however, he'd kept on his bedroom slippers—playing Auden, Maxine Dickey archly observed. Anyway, there in the photo Lowell is on the ground, knee up, hands on the weedy-looking grass, posing in front of his cousin Harriet Winslow's headstone in Washington, D.C.

Lowell's three-day visit to Columbia was sponsored by the university's student union, and I (as the student who invited him) played host. I didn't know it when we made that culminating pilgrimage, but thanks to Brown—his *Civil War Canon: Sites of Confederate Memory in South Carolina* (2015)—I now know, forty years later, that "Timrod's grave was an important symbolic site in the struggle over the postwar direction of the white South." I've also learned from Brown that Lowell "had theatrically fallen to his knees before the landmark," the granite boulder marking Timrod's grave. I think, Why not?

No doubt, as Kay Redfield Jamison asserts (in *Robert Lowell: Setting the River on Fire*), "New England was critical to how Lowell came to be." All the same, Lowell's Southern relations were extensive—a matter of blood as well as friendship and marriage. As familial connections deeply rooted in North Carolina may have inspired his diversion to Fort Sumter, perhaps his relationship with the Southern poets who were his mentors piqued an interest in Timrod.

Without a doubt, my Southern heritage had predisposed me to take an interest in "sites of Confederate memory." For me as a son of the South and a twenty-one-year-old aspiring poet, the pilgrimage to Timrod's grave with my favorite poet—with Robert Lowell, this self-conscious Bostonian (whose maternal grandmother hailed from the Carolinas)—stirred thoughts at once about my regional heritage and my literary one. Personally, reading "91 Revere Street," I could relate to Lowell, or so I made believe, feeling as I did "the egotistic, slightly paranoid apprehensions of an only child." (I was hardly "mentally ill.") But without quite consciously knowing so, I was "learning to live in history." (So Lowell says of himself in an altogether other context, the aftermath of a love affair, in *Notebook*.) "What is history?" he asks and answers: "What you cannot touch."

Why shouldn't Lowell at least have dropped to a knee? Except that he didn't. Still, behind "For the Union Dead," a personal poem occasioned by a public festival, stands "Ode to the Confederate Dead," a private, even "solipsistic" poem by Allen Tate; and behind Tate's "ode" there's Timrod's Parnassian "Ode" ("Sung on the Occasion of Decorating the Graves of the Confederate Dead, at Magnolia Cemetery, Charleston, S.C., 1867"). "An abolitionist counterpart" to Tate's "Ode to the Confederate Dead"—this is how Steven Gould Axelrod (in *Robert Lowell: Life and Art*) describes Lowell's poem. In fact, Tate's ironic ode doesn't so much as glance at slavery. "Counterpart" better describes the stance of Lowell's commemoration of the Union dead to Timrod's "Ode," which at least refers, if vaguely, to "a fallen cause" of which the Confederate dead are "martyrs" (though it's the "defeated valor" as embodied by those martyrs that Timrod celebrates). Timrod's "few war poems," writes F. O. Matthiessen in his introduction to *The Oxford Book of American Verse* (in which I first read Timrod's "Ode" when I was fifteen), "which state the Southern cause with deep conviction, endure with a classic hardness." At any rate, as Brown incisively shows, the lineage from Timrod's "Ode" to Tate's "Ode to the Confederate Dead" and to Lowell's "For the Union Dead" also includes Kevin Young's "For the Confederate Dead" and Natasha Trethewey's "Elegy for the Native Guards." Would Young or Trethewey have dropped to a knee at Timrod's grave? Or Bob Dylan? (In 2006 Timrod enjoyed a burst of fame when Dylan, in the album *Modern Times*, "sampled"—but did not "plagiarize"—as Robert Polito judiciously puts it, lines of Timrod's verse.) Point taken.

But Tate, for whom Timrod, according to Matthiessen, was "the best Southern poet of his time," was Lowell's principal mentor. "I can think of no pleasanter honor than to follow Tate, Warren and Miss Welty," read Lowell's reply to my invitation. The student-sponsored award, the University of South Carolina Award for Distinction in Literature, that was now bringing Lowell to South Carolina had brought Tate and Robert Penn Warren, another of Lowell's mentors, to the university in 1973. (Welty had received the award in absentia.) This reply of Lowell's had arrived from England, where he was now living with his third wife, Lady Caroline Blackwood, and experiencing a "second fatherhood" with their two-year-old son, Sheridan—England, where you couldn't get superhot mustard, or so Lowell later insisted. The return address was Milgate Park, Bearsted, Maidstone, Kent—a country house described by Lowell, impishly to Peter Taylor (a genteel Southerner with an ardor for houses), as "early eighteenth-century Palladian, and very Old South messy," while the "help" was "very unreliable, even dangerous, Old South help." The flimsy, blue "air letter" addressed to me was dated January 26. "Terrible to think," the letter continued, "(yet like the like the [sic] sun I see out the window coming glaringly through the gray cloud) it is now nearly forty years ago I first visited Allen Tate on the Cumberland and must have changed my life. I see," he added, "my image has misled; I meant the sun is what I see looking backward, the clouds are not the present but also what I see looking backward." That visit to Tate, who had read at the university the previous spring, took place in 1937 when Lowell, then a college sophomore, withdrew from Harvard and apprenticed himself to Tate, pitching a green umbrella tent from Sears on his lawn. Lowell vividly recounts the episode in "Visiting the Tates" (Allen and his wife, the novelist Caroline Gordon). Indoors, as this self-described young "puritan" and "abolitionist" observed, a Confederate flag hung above the fireplace. While sometimes wry, Lowell's account is self-deprecating and affectionate, even reverential to the older poet: "Like a torn cat, I was taken in [by Tate] when I needed help, and in a sense I have never left." His description of Tate's manner, as conveyed by his poems, relates as keenly to Lowell's own: "Out of splutter and shambling comes a killing eloquence"—and all the more so when he exclaims, "How often something smashes through the tortured joy of composition to strike the impossible bull's-eye!"

Lowell's letter to me—his reflection on how crucial to him was that visit to Tate—echoes an observation to Peter Taylor in 1973: "In solitary moments I remember that Allen more or less saved me, once in 1937 and then again in 1941–42." In 1942–43—Lowell is off a year—he was (along with his first wife, the novelist Jean Stafford) a

76

houseguest of Tate and Gordon, this time in Monteagle, Tennessee. There he labored at the poems that made up *Land of Unlikeness* (1944), poems whose subsequent revisions found their way into *Lord Weary's Castle* (1946), Lowell's first commercially published (and Pulitzer Prize-winning) collection.

Peter Taylor, a native Tennessean whose stories about the denizens of Nashville, Memphis, and St. Louis were enshrined in two volumes by The Library of America in 2017 (and who was awarded a Pulitzer Prize for his 1986 novel *A Summons to Memphis*), became Lowell's best friend for life when they were housemates at Kenyon College. (At Lowell's funeral Taylor read "Where the Rainbow Ends," the last poem in *Lord Weary's Castle*—the only deviation from the Episcopal liturgy.) There their housemaster, himself a Nashville native with a newly earned master's degree from Vanderbilt, was Randall Jarrell, and he also became a fast friend of Lowell's for life. To Kenyon they had all three—Jarrell, Taylor, and Lowell—followed John Crowe Ransom, who had been Tate's professor (and Jarrell's) at Vanderbilt, when he moved from Nashville to Gambier, Ohio, in 1938.

As Lowell's formative literary (as well as personal) friendships were with Southern boys, his principal mentors were all of them Southerners, and they had all contributed to the Agrarian symposium *I'll Take My Stand* (1930) and before that to *The Fugitive*, the poetry journal whose publication from 1922–1925 signaled a literary renascence in the South: Tate, Ransom, and Robert Penn Warren, whose student Lowell became at Louisiana State University in 1940. And it so happened that Lowell's Boston psychiatrist, who contrived to send the adolescent Lowell south (after the boy's fight with his father), had himself been one of the Fugitive poets. Of Merrill Moore, Lowell writes ambivalently (in a late poem, "Unwanted), "I will not admit / his Tennessee rattling saved my life."

I've wondered half-seriously if the old agrarian South, before the "city habits" of the Tates' cosmopolitan houseguests (the British novelist Ford Madox Ford; his companion, the painter Janice Biala; and her sister, Ford's secretary) "exhausted the only cistern"—I've wondered if that Old South on the Cumberland isn't somewhere in the old South Boston aquarium's "dark downward and vegetating kingdom /

of the fish and reptile" for which Lowell "often sigh[s] still," sighs because the "airy tanks are dry" and "Parking spaces luxuriate like civic / sandpiles" and "giant finned cars nose forward like fish" and the culture, a desiccated urban culture, subsisting as it does on industry and commerce, sees as its "Rock of Ages" a "Mosler Safe."

If Moore's "Tennessee rattling" maybe saved his life and that visit to Tate on the Cumberland "must" have done so, what of his marriage to Elizabeth Hardwick, who "faced the kingdom of the mad— / its hackneyed speech, its homicidal eye— / and dragged [him] home alive"? Hardwick hailed from Kentucky. So what if "the shrill verve of [her] invective scorched the traditional South"! Still she was a "Southern belle," at least by Tate's reckoning, and so by extension was the couple's daughter. As Tate, in one of Lowell's *Notebook* sonnets, tipsily insists to child Harriet, "*You* are a Southern *belle*; do you know why / you are a *Southern* belle?...Because you *mother* is a Southern belle."

I had wondered, ahead of Lowell's visit, if the mad Lowell, "Cal" as Caligula, would show. When I shared with my roommate the author's photograph (by Fay Godwin) on the jacket flap of *History*, which views, straight on but off center, the long-haired poet from waist up (sport shirt unironed), in front of a manor house, Milgate Park—head slightly bowed, making eye-contact through the top half of black frames—"A demented dwarf," my roommate responded. At the airport I'm surprised by how tall Lowell is. "I'm only a fraction over six feet," he murmurs. We've left the concourse and he's loping, head down, toward the convenience store for gum. "You must have quit smoking," I say. He shoots a glance my way. "How did you know?" I didn't, of course. I might have remembered that he "chain-smoked through the night" in "Eye and Tooth," a poem that Lowell later reads to his South Carolina audience, "learning to flinch / at the flash of the matchlight," but instead I'm picturing the throwaway lighter's inches-tall flare in that *Encyclopaedia Britannica* film about James Dickey, *Lord, Let Me Die But Not Die Out*, the segment filmed in Lowell's New York City apartment, as Lowell lights a Salem. (The film takes as its title the conclusion of Dickey's poem about extinction, "For the Last Wolverine," which is also his *ars poetica*.)

I do know, however, that Lowell is not drinking. After he informed me in a telegram that he'd be arriving from Monteagle, which the Dickeys understood to mean Nashville, but at what time he did not say, Maxine discovered that he had decamped from Tate's Monteagle, Tennessee, to Peter Taylor's Charlottesville, Virginia, and there she'd phoned ostensibly to find out what was Lowell's drink of choice but really, of course, to find out whence and when he'd be arriving. Anyway, he wasn't drinking because of his medications. (At this time, according to Hamilton, Lowell was taking Antabuse for alcohol abuse.)

It was scary, nonetheless—Lowell's enthusiasm for the mustard. He's sitting across from me in a booth at a Chinese restaurant near the university—across from me and my friend and fellow student Jim Mann—scooping it up with fried wontons, which came with the pu-pu platter, gobs of sinus-eviscerating mustard, while Jim and I eye each other with anxious incredulity. "You can't get mustard like this in England," Lowell marvels.

But if Lowell's own madness didn't present, an avatar of madness did—and presented himself to Lowell and unnerved him. There was, following the reading, a reception at Capstone House, a high-rise women's dorm. Lowell had already been discomfited, on the elevator up, by a stranger claiming kin, who unrolled an elaborate family tree, which he pressed a suspicious and, as the elevator stopped and the doors began to part, a begrudgingly obliging Lowell to sign. I've only begun to edge my way into the crowded lounge when a fellow student is tapping me on the shoulder—"Mr. Lowell wants you"—right as Lowell himself is asking through the crowd, "Where's Mr. Havird?" Beleaguered he sounds. He's on his feet in front of the sofa where he was sitting—wanting to leave. Only as we are exiting the dorm—as I open the glass door for us to exit the lobby—does Lowell speak. "I was sitting next to a madman," he says, with an accent on each syllable: *mad man*. "Yes, I know," I say. Jim Mann remembers this fellow well— remembers that he, like Lowell, took Lithium for manic-depression. Remembers his fury when Jim "criticized him for revising endlessly" a poem that Dickey praised in class "instead of writing another." "Seriously intelligent, he recited more great poems by heart to me than anyone else I've ever known." Jim describes this fellow's recitation of *Hugh Selwyn Mauberley*, "the approving smile on his face when he spoke the lines: 'The case presents / No adjunct to the Muses' diadem.'" Remembers him as the "one authentically 'crazy poet'" he's "truly known." This madman—picture the actor Richard Kiel; picture him as Jaws, the nemesis of Roger Moore's James Bond—had sidled up next to Lowell on the sofa. "He wanted to know"—and in spite of Lowell's bewilderment persisted in wanting to know—"why I had tried to electrocute Ezra Pound," Lowell nervously explains.

He'd faced himself "the kingdom of the mad"; now he was en route to a party at the Dickeys'. I did not know it then, but in a 1967 letter to Elizabeth Bishop, Lowell had described "the optimistic James Dickey" as "one of the most desperate souls I know of," and in 1969, after "assisting" in that *Britannica* film, quoted Dickey as saying, "my problems are worse than yours." "They are," Lowell agreed. Be that as it may, when told about Lowell's encounter with the madman, Dickey relates an incident in class—that in response to some innocuous, factual statement like "Tennyson was a Victorian poet," there came from the back of the room, from this Jaws, a sort of drawling rumble, "Bullshit," of sufficient menace that Dickey, a lifelong athlete whom you could see stringing that bow of Ulysses, began to fear for his physical safety.

If Lowell's daughter, Harriet, was a Southern belle because her mother was (Elizabeth Hardwick, who "snatched me out of chaos," as Lowell acknowledged in his hand-printed inscription to Lizzie in *Day by Day* one month before he died), then by Tate's logic so was Lowell's mother a Southern belle, this woman by whom he was so determined not to be "mastered" that he saw his manic self, according to Jamison, as the rebel who was able to "relive his battles with his mother and win them." Mania, Jamison reports, quoting from Lowell's 1949 Payne Whitney Clinic medical records, "allowed him to vent his rage at being 'fixed in society'…; it allowed him to escape the 'dreariness of being a Lowell.'" And *her* mother—Charlotte Winslow Lowell's mother— Mary Devereux Winslow (the Mary Winslow whom Lowell's syntax in the elegy for her in *Lord Weary's Castle* identifies as "the bestial cow" on Boston Common) hailed from Raleigh, North Carolina, where her

80

father, John Devereux, Jr., was a planter who farmed with his father. According to the *Dictionary of North Carolina Biography,* between them they owned some 1500 slaves. During the Civil War, Lowell's maternal great-grandfather was the Confederate quartermaster general for North Carolina. In 1943, horrified by the cost in civilian lives of "an almost apocalyptic series of all-out air raids" on Hamburg, Lowell resisted the draft and in a dutiful note to that grandmother, which accompanied a copy of his public "Declaration of Personal Responsibility," observed, "only a Southerner can realize the horrors of a merciless conquest." Mary Devereux had married a New Englander whose English forebears had "furiously" supported the Puritan Oliver Cromwell, and "in her heart," her grandson speculates (in "Antebellum Boston," a posthumously published essay), "she may have decided that her husband's 'kind'"—well-satisfied, overbearing, strict—"was at fault" for the American Civil War. Grandmother Winslow "could never quite swallow New England." Mariani reports that Lowell had been looking for Devereux connections in and around Raleigh immediately before his sightseeing tour of Charleston and Fort Sumter.

"I'm Southern," Lowell asserts in a 1958 letter to Tate.

Now, maybe he's slyly recalling that when he pitched that tent on the Cumberland, he was judged by Tate to be "an idealist New Englander, a Puritan"—an avatar of Yankee intellect, which abstracted from the whole while the Southern mind embraced its complex particularity. (As if there was no such creature as a Southern ideologue!) But if there's irony in Lowell's Southern claim, no doubt there's also sincere emotion, whether or not he has his Southern lineage in mind: Lowell felt, as he tells Ian Hamilton, that as a result of his jail time for conscientious objection, he "had a more Southern wholeness."

Whether Lowell's Southern heritage was in his thoughts at Timrod's grave I do not know. But he did not genuflect, much less "theatrically" fall to his knees. "Turn your eyes to the immoderate past," Tate says in "Ode to the Confederate Dead." At Timrod's grave Lowell might as well have been at Fort Sumter, hearkening to Tate's imperative but seeing in place of an "inscrutable infantry rising / Demons out of the earth" only "coastal desert." He might have been prompted to kneel by an "active faith," by "knowledge / Carried to the heart"; but perhaps, "in the fragmentary cosmos of today," it was unavailable to Lowell as earlier even to Tate. (Here I piece together phrases from Tate's essay, "Narcissus as Narcissus," about his "Ode" as well as from the "Ode" itself.)

"Your *Elegy* is not for the Confederate dead, but for your own dead emotion," Tate's fellow Fugitive Donald Davidson, a Southern ideologue, wrote in 1927, and Tate, without exactly disagreeing, replied, "if I have a living emotion about a dead one…isn't that enough for a poem?" "Ode to the Confederate Dead" is an interior monologue in which Tate gives voice to three perspectives: there is first the presiding consciousness, an eye that takes in the scene, the rows of headstones that "yield their names to the element," the wind; then there is *you*, for whom that consciousness interprets the scene (the "thousand acres where these memories grow / From the inexhaustible bodies that are not / Dead, but feed the grass row after rich row"), to whom he speaks imperatives ("Turn your eyes to the immoderate past, / Turn to the inscrutable infantry rising"), and whose intuitions he channels ("Demons out of the earth—they will not last"). It is this *you* who personifies that dead emotion about Southern valor to which Davidson refers.

Finally, there is *we*—"we who…bow / Our heads with a commemorial woe / In the ribboned coats of grim felicity"—a social remnant that "has knowledge carried to the heart," a remnant, in other words, for whom the chivalric ideal abides if not quite as an active faith (because the Old South has been defeated not only by Federal troops but also by scientific naturalism), then as a twilit thing of occasional veneration—the Lost Cause, "a grave / In the house"—by an ever inward-turning cult. Call this cult the Sons of Confederate Veterans, who do have occasion to dress up in beribboned gray coats, or the United Daughters of the Confederacy, among whom count my father's older sister, my Aunt Mabel (a willowy maiden aunt, whose image, when I first encountered Lowell's Aunt Sarah Stark Winslow in *Life Studies*, "a beauty too lofty and original ever to marry," took shape in my mind—alabaster skin, rose cheeks, red hair).

"Shiloh, Antietam, Malvern Hill, Bull Run"—as a boy whose favorite toy was his "Giant Blue and Gray Battle Set," which consisted of blue and gray plastic soldiers and yellowish-ivory-colored plastic effigies of Lincoln and Grant, Jefferson Davis and Lee, plastic cannons that shot forth pellets by means of a metal trigger-like spring, brown plastic *chevaux de frise* (not that I knew then the term for those spikes), green plastic two-dimensional trees...I'd lose myself "in that orient of the thick-and-fast"—as though, but only as though, I had a personal stake in the outcome. After all, my great-grandfather, born in 1835, and two of his brothers lost their lives defending the Cause. (Slaveholders were they? The Havirds, my father insisted, were too poor to own slaves. An oft-heard Southern claim.) An infantryman, Wilson Havird was mortally wounded—in what battle I do not know. Discharged, this great-grandfather of mine engendered a child, my grandfather, born in 1864, a posthumous baby, who later, from 1899–1923, sired ten children, the fifth of whom, born in 1909, was my father. These children had as play-money Confederate dollar bills. Once, an uncle of mine presented me with a Confederate ten-dollar bill. Unsuccessfully I rummaged my grandmother's house, the outbuildings too (in one of which there were wreaths from my grandfather's funeral in 1944), for the stash.

On my mother's side there was a whole generation's difference—that is to say, my maternal great-grandfather was born in the very same year as that paternal great-grandfather succumbed to his wounds: 1864. His name: William Sherman Belk. As my mother told the story, General Sherman had himself come to the house—for what reason, I don't remember knowing—discovered that there was a baby, and asked what was its name. A baby boy, he hadn't yet been named. The General responded, "Why not name him 'William Sherman'?"—an apparently casual suggestion, which the family inexplicably followed. Only after the boy had started school and a teacher told him what a "terrible" man Sherman had been (my mother's word, "terrible"), only then did he begin to go by "Billy," as he was for the rest of his life, until his obituary appeared in 1916, a notice that includes his manner of death, a violent altercation with a "negro," whom he was supervising as the "Good Road Overseer," and there he is William Sherman Belk.

Lately I've discovered that when Sherman set up camp in and around Cheraw, a town in South Carolina some ninety miles northeast of Columbia (the capital, which burned after surrendering to Sherman in February 1865), this as-yet-unnamed infant boy, born in March 1864, was turning one year old. A first cousin of my mother's had understood from her mother, one of Billy's daughters, that the family had deferred naming him so long as the father, who joined the Confederate army in 1863, was off engaging the Yankees. Had this Rebel soldier returned by early March 1865? I had wondered if the family wasn't Unionist or entirely outside history. (In fact, the rebel in me, the lowercase rebel, had slyly relished the thought.) Anyway, after three days Sherman resumed his march. Was there a christening in the meantime? Surely the Belks were Baptist, and Baptists don't hold to infant baptism. However, the year-old infant's Christian name, William Sherman, held. Where's the family Bible!

So, there I'd be, a child on the hardwood floor of his bedroom, where the rug didn't reach, setting up those plastic soldiers, the Blue and the Gray—amid them those green trees and gray skeletal ones and in front of either side those cannons to blast it apart. Which among those graycoats, that "infantry rising," were the Havirds? Envision them I may have done—"Demons out of the earth." If so, the vision did not last. Whatever knowledge I had or have accrued of my personal link to the Confederacy—I haven't carried it to heart.

As neither had Lowell—taken to heart, I mean, knowledge of his own Confederate ties, ties of blood to the South's "immoderate past." Because he knew that Southern chivalry was "shit"? (In *Notebook* his Orestes "knew that Trojan chivalry was shit" while anticipating the execution of Clytemnestra, his monstrous mother, a sometime stand-in for Lowell's own.)

Until now I have myself never written in verse or prose about my Confederate heritage. The poem of mine that emerged from my engagement with Lowell, "Midnight Oil"—the earliest written of my published poems, composed within months of this pilgrimage to Timrod's grave—paid stylistic homage to Lowell as a pastiche in particular of "Night Sweat" and the stanza in "Beyond the Alps," the first poem in *Life Studies*, that Lowell restored "at the suggestion of John Berryman" for its subsequent publication in *For the Union Dead*. While Lowell "thought of Ovid," I "think of Swinburne" (if only because he was an upper-class rebel against Victorian piety). For me, "learning to live in history" became "living in *literary* history"—as may have been true for Lowell, whose *History* is populated by as many literary figures (not least of all himself) as political ones. Twenty years after its publication in *Poetry* in November 1976, "Midnight Oil" underwent substantial revision, as did individual lines before the new version's 2013 publication in *Map Home* (amid a cluster of poems in which I'm on a literary pilgrimage). Even now I find myself "knotting, undoing" that poem's "fishnet of tarred rope," as Lowell, in *The Dolphin*, describes his own obsessive revising.

Perhaps for Lowell it wasn't Southern chivalry alone but ideology more broadly that failed to root, to grip the heart, because a "mania for phrases" had "dried" it. Or rather, on second thought, "enlarged his heart." As with his paragon Flaubert, to whom Lowell attributes this mania, so with Lowell himself. (I quote from two versions of the same sonnet: "*Les Mots*" in *Notebook*, "First Love" in *History*.)

Lowell was flying out in the afternoon. With the morning to kill, Jim Mann suggested a pilgrimage to Timrod's grave. It was near the university, in Trinity Episcopal churchyard, across the street from the Capitol. From the Sumter Street entrance, we could see, on the statehouse grounds, the equestrian statue of Wade Hampton, a Confederate general, governor, and United States senator—a champion of the "Lost Cause"—who also rests in peace in Trinity churchyard. Make the pilgrimage today, forty years later, and you can just discern, past the Palmetto trees, magnolias, and azaleas, the African American Monument, which tells the black South Carolinian story.

With its bronze bas relief there on the statehouse grounds, a pilgrimage undertaken today to Timrod's grave would call even more vividly to mind than in 1974 Lowell's "Colonel Shaw / and his bell-cheeked Negro infantry / on St. Gaudens'…Civil War relief" facing the Massachusetts statehouse. In Lowell's poem, the bronze faces of the Negroes, who seemed to William James to breathe, anticipate, eight stanzas later, "the drained faces of Negro school-children" on television, which "rise like balloons." Sixty years separate the dedication of the monument in 1897 from the federally enforced desegregation of Little Rock Central High School in 1957, which Lowell may have in mind. Meanwhile, almost a century after the unsuccessful assault on

Fort Wagner, Colonel Shaw "is riding on his bubble," his dream of racial equality, as then he "rode" his troops. As they did then, now the children embody the dream. At the beginning of the poem there are bubbles "drifting from the noses of the cowed, compliant fish," which Lowell as a boy "tingled" to burst. Now, as the children's faces on TV are "drained," so the TV-like tanks, which held those fish, are "dry." And anyway, the bubbles only seemed to drift from their noses, as the bronze infantrymen only seemed to breathe, coming as those bubbles did from air pumps, aerating the water. Has the dream of racial equality, which the bubbles come to symbolize, been merely a dream, an illusion? It is a dream so long deferred that its avatars, the schoolchildren who have replaced the infantrymen, are exhausted, as is the colonel, who "waits / for the blessèd break."

As Lowell may be too, however he may "lament the loss of the old Abolitionist spirit": exhausted, or "withered." *For the Union Dead*, said Lowell, who wrote it while depressed—the "whole book [is] about witheredness." At the end of the title poem, "giant finned cars nose forward like fish." But not like the fish that Lowell remembers from his boyhood at the beginning of the poem, "the cowed, compliant fish." Now "a savage servility / slides by on grease." Think Caliban (another of Lowell's "namesakes"), who smells like a fish. Anyway, that epithet, "savage servility," applies as well to drivers as to cars, those drivers lacking an animating ideal (like racial equality) for whom the Cadillac has come to symbolize the American Dream. Sigh he may "for the dark downward and vegetating kingdom" of those fish, but here is Lowell, as he depicts himself in "Returning" (another poem in *For the Union Dead*), "rushed / by the green go-light of those nervous waters" of his personal odyssey—from the old South Boston Aquarium to the Cumberland River to Charleston harbor, as well as within his psyche— as though behind the wheel of one of those finned cars, where "I found / my exhaustion, the light of the world."

The dedication in 2001 of South Carolina's African American Monument followed the lowering of the Confederate battle flag from the Capitol dome, where it had flown (in commemoration of the hundredth anniversary of the Rebel bombardment of Fort Sumter) since April 1961. It then went up on a pole beside the Confederate

Monument, a granite obelisk on top of which the abstract Confederate soldier daydreams over his musket, facing north. In 2015, after the massacre of nine African American church-goers in Charleston by a twenty-year-old white supremacist who had brandished a Rebel flag in photos, the flag came down—went into storage somewhere. In 1974, of course, the battle flag was flying atop the statehouse, below the indigo-blue state flag with its white palmetto tree and crescent moon, below the Stars and Stripes.

Timrod's grave lies in a modest family plot enclosed by a waist-high wrought-iron fence, a stone's throw from the street, Gervais, a noisy four-lane street, that crosses Main in front of the Capitol. Born in Charleston in 1829, Timrod died in Columbia of tuberculosis in 1867, right as the decade of Radical Reconstruction began. The poet's "memorial boulder," as Brown points out, dates from 1901, thanks to a campaign by a former Charleston mayor (and Timrod revivalist) whose intent was "to evoke...the piece of New England granite that Emerson had chosen to mark his grave in Concord."

Outside the fence, in front of that boulder, my friend, Jim Mann, brought forth from his shoulder bag a copy of the 1899 memorial edition of Timrod's *Poems* with its introductory memoir by Timrod's friend and fellow poet Paul Hamilton Hayne. What Jim read was not a Parnassian poem by Timrod but an overwrought, eulogistic passage of Hayne's:

> On 7 October, the mortal remains of the poet, so worn and shattered, were buried in the cemetery of Trinity Church, Columbia.
>
> There, in the ruined capital of his native State, whence scholarship, culture, and social purity have been banished to give place to the orgies of semi-barbarians and the political trickery of adventurers and traitors; there, tranquil amid the vulgar turmoil of factions, reposes the dust of one of the truest and sweetest singers this country has given to the world.

That phrase—what was that phrase? Lowell is rummaging the pockets of his blue suit for a piece of paper, a scrap, which he now unfolds from his wallet. Fazed or not by the sexual racism, silver ballpoint pen in hand, "Tranquil amid the vulgar turmoil of factions," he prints (able as he is to write in cursive two words only: "Robert" and "Lowell"). "You can use that anywhere," he murmurs.

His accent was eerily Southern.

WITH ARCHIBALD MACLEISH
OUTSIDE DEBRUHL'S CAFÉ

"Hello, Archie." The tone is at once sly and familiar, slyly familiar. Archibald MacLeish, a quizzical expression on his face, looks up. James Dickey closes in and grasps his hand.

In April 1975, when my wife and I were twenty-one-year-old undergraduate sweethearts, we played host at the University of South Carolina to Archibald MacLeish, who was there to receive a literary award we students had created. For his part, at the ceremony, this octogenarian poet played ancient Mariner to us students' Wedding Guest. "My best to James Dickey," MacLeish had concluded when accepting the invitation. Dickey was the poet-in-residence and our teacher. Ashley Mace and I were both aspiring writers, and I at least was trying out voices and stances, brands of cigarettes and Scotch, and even headwear. "I hope he can be there," and Dickey was; and Allen Tate was there in name: "Columbia rings with his name and fame," MacLeish later observed.

In the Dickeys' living room, with its floor-to-ceiling bookshelves, there is a stack of MacLeish's books for the poet to sign. "To James Dickey," he writes, "man and poet." Dickey played football at Clemson, MacLeish at Yale; Dickey saw combat in World War Two, MacLeish in World War One. Doubtless MacLeish finds in Dickey's person no less than in his poetry a masculine, athletic physicality that he relates to, that impresses him.

"I thought he'd be a lot taller," Dickey later says. He had not previously met Archie. He recalls the photographs of MacLeish outdoors in *The Dialogues of Archibald MacLeish and Mark Van Doren* in which MacLeish is wearing a short-sleeved knit shirt that shows off his athlete's chest and arms. "Because of his long face," I suggest—the long upper lip and chin, high forehead, Roman nose.

Only in his temples, when he removes his navy blue beret, where there are crinkly veins and freckles, does MacLeish look at all his age, and then only amid the fluorescent lighting of the elevator at the motel where we lodged him in the reddest room he'd ever seen. With its red satin drapes and billowy valence and quilted bedspread, it looked, I said, like a bordello in a Western; and he—he wasn't himself going to say so. One month shy of eighty-three, MacLeish looks fit. He swims, MacLeish later explains to Ashley.

Despite that stack of books, Dickey doesn't know "exactly what to think about MacLeish." So he says in an in-class lecture posthumously edited by his colleague Donald Greiner: "He has a slender but very genuine lyric talent, but he also has, or has had, a right-wing rhetorical stance, which makes him less and less popular." Whatever his *rhetorical* stance may be, MacLeish's politics are New Deal liberal. In fact, when appointed librarian of Congress by President Roosevelt in 1939, MacLeish became, thanks to his condemnation by a Republican congressman, the first "fellow traveler"—someone who associated with Communists even if he didn't himself belong to the party. Dickey echoes left-wing attacks by Edmund Wilson and Dwight Macdonald, among others, on MacLeish as the author of "The Irresponsibles" (1940), a "controversial pamphlet," as the editors of *The Norton Anthology of Modern Poetry* describe it, that "charged the great writers of his generation with weakening the moral fiber of their readers and leaving them prey to Fascism." Using that anthology, published in 1973 and still new in 1975, to prepare my introduction of MacLeish at the award ceremony, I confide beforehand that I won't be mentioning "The Irresponsibles." Why ever not? he asks—he's very proud of "The Irresponsibles." Not to belittle the magnitude of the slaughter—after all, it took the life of his younger brother—but World War One, MacLeish insists, was a "commercial war"; World War Two was "Armageddon."

Dickey does, however, commend the poems: "You, Andrew Marvell" as "one of the most beautiful poems that the English tongue has ever conceived of" and "Epistle to Be Left in the Earth" for its "haunting cadence," which is distinctively *MacLeish*. (Apart from "Ars Poetica"—"A poem should not mean / But be"—"You, Andrew Marvell" is *the* poem that represents MacLeish in anthologies.) "MacLeish is one of the few American poets who ever really had a voice," Dickey observes many years later, in 1992, when I am reviewing *Archibald MacLeish: An American Life* by Scott Donaldson for *The Virginia Quarterly Review*. "His is a kind of Anglo-Saxon elegiac Americanized voice, very sad and nostalgic and very masculine: the kind of poetry Hemingway might have written if Hemingway had been able to write poetry." Compare Dickey's gesture at Hemingway to Allen Tate's observation in 1932 about "the clarity of sensuous reminiscence that suffuses the entire poem," *Conquistador*, MacLeish's long poem about the Spanish conquest of the Aztecs: "it has appeared in this age only in the prose of Ernest Hemingway, chiefly in the opening pages of *A Farewell to Arms*."

"You, Andrew Marvell" and "Epistle to Be Left in the Earth" both appeared in *New Found Land*, a collection of fourteen poems published in 1930, the culmination of MacLeish's intentional "education as a poet," whose campus had been Paris. There he had moved in 1923 and lived for five years with his wife and their two small children. "I thought MacLeish's new book very good. Well, even better than that," wrote John Peale Bishop to Allen Tate in August 1930. "He has at last shaken off the sand of the Waste Land from his feet and written at least three poems that are about as good as one gets." As to that debt to *The Waste Land*, no doubt Bishop had in mind *The Pot of Gold* (1925), its mythopoeic framework and verbal echoes. Which three poems those were that "are about as good as one gets" Bishop neglected to specify: let's say in addition to "You, Andrew Marvell" and "Epistle to Be Left in the Earth" "'Not Marble Nor the Gilded Monuments.'" "I think he is without any doubt writing the best poetry written in America, and that he has the biggest future," Ernest Hemingway wrote in December 1930, pitching MacLeish to Maxwell Perkins at Scribner's. "Some of the poetry that he's written all ready [*sic*] will be good a couple hundred years from now as it is."

But in 1923, when MacLeish quit the practice of law in Boston to practice the art of poetry in Paris, he was by his own admission "totally ignorant of the new challenge to the poetic tradition that had been opened largely by Pound and Eliot." In Paris MacLeish learned Italian and so read Dante's *Commedia*. Later in *Conquistador*, MacLeish's innovative accentual meter and use of assonance in place of rhyme in its three-line stanzas resulted in a "fluent rapidity and ease" that rivaled, in Tate's judgment, those qualities in "the best Italian *terza rima*. It is the first successful example of this stanza in a long English poem," Tate asserted. MacLeish read *Anabase* by St.-John Perse in French and right away, in 1926 (when Eliot was beginning his translation), sensed it to be one of those "three or four books in a writer's life which are like the changes of direction in a long valley" and its author his "blood brother." So he raved in a letter to Princess Bassiano. And in Arthur Waley's translations, he read, among other Chinese poets, Po Chü-i (Bai Juyi), to whom he refers in "American Letter," the longest of the fourteen poems in *New Found Land*, that "touchstone text on questions of place," as the poet and scholar H. R. Stoneback describes it, "a benchmark of expatriate meditation." I've never read Chinese poetry, I tell MacLeish in conversation. "You must!" he insists. "Read Waley; he's better than Pound"—the Pound, that is, of *Cathay*.

Nevertheless, while in law school at Harvard, newly married and needing money, MacLeish had tutored Yale men on Shakespeare and Milton, and Milton it was that inspired the mysterious, puzzling final line of "Epistle to Be Left in the Earth": "Voices are crying an unknown name in the sky." In Book 4 of *Paradise Lost* Adam explains to Eve that there are unseen millions of angels on earth and they "with ceaseless praise…behold" God's new creation: "how often…have we heard / Celestial voices to the midnight air…Singing thir great Creator" (lines 679–684). In MacLeish's poem the "name" is "unknown" because "none among us have seen God": "We have thought often / The flaws of sun in the late and driving weather / Pointed to one tree but it was not so." And as for those voices in the sky, "They are not words at all," the epistle insists, "but the wind rising."

In a 1932 letter to Tate, MacLeish ponders why "generation after generation of poets" should "record such facts as the fact that tilled earth has a certain smell, that dark comes late in summer, that men at midnight think of such and such things" and concludes that this question, the subject of "Epistle to Be Left in the Earth," has "no answer." However "strange" may be the "compulsion," its aim, as MacLeish comes to see and insists twenty years later to his student the novelist Ilona Karmel, is not only to "testify" that "we are here" but also to "praise." Meanwhile, in "Epistle to Be Left in the Earth" the poet testifies on behalf us descendents of Cain whose compensation for the loss of God is a laborious discovery of things of the earth as worthy of praise—praiseworthy because of their elemental materiality, and praiseworthy despite our apprehension of doom and rumors, numinous or not, that haunt us when night is "very cold."

Years later, reminiscing with Dickey about MacLeish's visit, I marvel at a phrase in an earlier poem, "Memorial Rain": "the thin grating / Of ants under the grass," which conveys the point of view of the buried soldier, MacLeish's younger brother Kenneth. About MacLeish's trip in 1924 from Paris to Flanders Field for the official dedication of the cemetery, "Memorial Rain" displays MacLeish's mastery of form and rhetoric. The poem cuts back and forth from the ceremony, which MacLeish satirizes by indirectly quoting the ambassador's vapid, formulaic testimonial, to the poet's private, emotionally controlled response, which tracks the changing weather. The *terza rima* ought to hasten the event, but those cinematic cuts from the ambassador's remarks in present time to the poet's retrospective description of his journey create suspense—until the last line brings relief: "And suddenly, and all at once, the rain!" Dickey's mind is elsewhere: "'Epistle to Be Left in the Earth,'" he says, "is one of the greatest poems written in any language."

From that book-walled living room, Mrs. Dickey, Maxine, herds us—MacLeish and Dickey, Jim Mann, the graduate student whose brainchild was this literary award, and Ashley and me—into the adjacent den. You can see out the picture window the pine-treed back yard, where an archery target leans against a tree, and beyond this Lake Katharine. There's a dock, and when I'm out at the Dickeys' some time later, I will find Dickey sitting there and nursing a sixteen-ounce can of Miller High Life with sextants and other to-me-mysterious instruments beside him on the wooden bench and at his feet, his bare feet with their diseased toenails. I remember then my first time with Dickey outside of class, at a hotdog restaurant near the university. Dickey recited from "The Rime of the Ancient Mariner" (lines 25–28):

93

The sun came up upon the left,
Out of the sea came he!
And he shone bright, and on the right
Went down into the sea...

then pointedly asked in which direction was the Mariner sailing.
"South," I said and felt as though I'd passed a crucial test. With that
image in mind of Dickey on the dock amid those nautical, navigational
instruments, I ask him many years later why he hadn't made the pro-
tagonist of *The Zodiac*, his disappointing long poem about a drunken
poet's desperate attempt "to relate himself, by means of the stars, to the
universe," a Southern suburbanite instead of a Dutchman and set it
beside a manmade lake instead of amid the canals of Amsterdam. "Next
time!" he says. We situate ourselves—MacLeish and Dickey, Jim Mann
and Ashley and I—in steel-and-black-leather Wassily-style chairs
around a huge glass-topped knee-high table. Maxine serves Bloody
Marys.

Dickey has only recently completed *The Zodiac*, which is based on
a poem by the Dutch poet Hendrik Marsman. With some enthusiasm
Dickey describes *The Zodiac* for MacLeish much as I've done above by
quoting from the prefatory note to the 1976 Doubleday edition. If
MacLeish could know that *The Zodiac* in its limited edition would fea-
ture this epigraph by Neil Armstrong—"The earth is travelling...in the
direction of the constellation Hercules to some unknown destination
in the cosmos"—he might appear even more enthralled. "There are
many stars," he writes in "Epistle to Be Left in the Earth," "we are
drifting / North by the Great Bear." But when Dickey informs us that
The Zodiac will be coming out in *Playboy*, MacLeish, as he later con-
fides, is appalled. In fact, the poem appears nowhere in print until a
local publisher of reference books issues that limited edition in September 1976.

Among MacLeish's poems "The Reef Fisher" is one of Dickey's
personal favorites. Won't MacLeish read it, Dickey asks. He explains
that for a long time his younger son, now in high school and a basket-
ball star, was sea-obsessed. (Dickey, who seems to have wanted to stay

a nineteen-year-old jock forever, according to his older son, Christopher, has begun feeling very competitive toward Kevin.) Dickey even addressed a poem to the boy: "Giving a Son to the Sea." "Gentle blondness and the moray eel go at the same time / On in my mind as you grow...Your room is full / Of flippers and snorkels and books / On spearfishing." Dickey's poem has an ecological theme: the need for human beings, due to a population explosion, to adapt to life undersea. It also offers a parable of a parent's letting go as the child matures toward a darkly unfamiliar life apart. MacLeish's poem "The Reef Fisher," Dickey implies, is a special favorite of his because it's also a favorite poem of Kevin's. And, as Dickey points out in that in-class lecture, "it's in that exquisite MacLeishian cadence."

"The Reef Fisher" is also one of maybe a dozen later poems whose imagery connects them to MacLeish's winters on Antigua. Some of these, notably "Calypso's Island," appear in the Pulitzer Prize-winning 1952 *Collected Poems*; others, notably "Dr. Sigmund Freud Discovers the Sea Shell," in *Songs for Eve* (1954), MacLeish's best book of all new poems after *New Found Land*. There on that island in the West Indies, MacLeish played croquet and drank rum punch with wealthy fellow members of the Mill Reef Club while honing anew, after a decade in Washington that "silenced" him "as a poet," the craft of poetry, an enterprise that must have mystified those corporate executives much as it did my father. It pleased my father to meet MacLeish since here was a poet who'd had a career in government service such as he, an attorney with the Veterans Administration, could envision for his would-be poet son.

Obviously moved by Dickey's request, MacLeish obliges in an accent of cultivated, dulcet lyricism. He observes by the way that "The Reef Fisher" is dedicated and spoken to his own son Kenneth, who is a SCUBA-diver. (This, the poet's older son, the eldest of his three children, is named, of course, for MacLeish's younger brother, the naval aviator shot down and killed in World War One.) The poem's scenario is archetypal, its symbolism fusing elements from two mythological narratives: the quest of Jason for the Golden Fleece and of Perseus for the head of Medusa. In the poem the son is spearfishing—the object of his quest is "the fabulous / Fish of fishes" (the poem's Golden Fleece,

signifying such masculine attributes as wealth and regal authority)—
while the poet-father addresses to him a series of encouraging imperatives and then this warning: to "fear that weed, as though alive, / That
lifts and follows with the wave"—

> The Moray lurks for all who dive
> Too deep within the coral cave.
> Once tooth of his has touched the bone
> Men turn among those stones to stone.

The last two lines, in which the moray eel becomes a tress of the Gor-
gon as well as the wakeful dragon with its martial teeth guarding the
Golden Fleece—those lines, MacLeish reveals, have now for him a
painful poignancy: this son, a senior editor of *National Geographic*, suf-
fers from bone cancer.

Two years later, a letter from MacLeish (September 5, 1977) in
reply to one of mine begins: "Thank you for the vivid account of your
Grand Tour which reached me a little before our world fell apart."
(That Grand Tour of Ashley's and mine had taken us in five weeks
from England, through France, to Italy.) A follow-up note explains:
"My son Kenneth died on August 5 after five years of agony. Bone
Cancer. I think you told me once you knew my poem called the Reef
Fisher [*sic*]." To MacLeish the warning that concludes the poem seems
to have been uncannily prophetic, maybe even indicative of blame—
as if that prophetic warning, while expressive of paternal care, masked
the father's competitive stance toward the son.

Such a Freudian interpretation is encouraged by MacLeish's
younger son William's description (in *Uphill with Archie: A Son's Journey*) of the sometimes fractious relationship between the father and his
older son. To Bill, the baby in the family, the friction derived from the
soldier father's absence from home during World War One when Kenneth was an infant. When he returned, the boy was "a talking toddler":
"When Captain MacLeish came back, Kenny took one look at the
stranger with the uniform and the mustache and said, 'It is not a dog-
gie.' The son had had his mother all to himself for months, while the

father had nothing but letters to ease his yearnings. The two males, small and tall, looked at each other and growled."

If James Dickey was there for MacLeish's visit, Allen Tate was too—if only in name. "I am writing Tate to tell him Columbia rings with his name and fame," MacLeish informs me after his visit. "'When Tate was here!'" he marvels. My contribution to Tate's fame was to quote Robert Lowell, who asks of Tate in one of his *Notebook* sonnets, "Who else would sire twins at sixty-eight"; or rather to misquote Lowell, substituting "could" for "would." "Any man could," MacLeish snapped. I'd meant to be amusingly salacious, remembering as I was that during Tate's reading at the university in 1973, George Garrett had kept thinking distractedly, "Here was the satyr of the age."

Quite apart from Garrett's quip, that reading of Tate's had been a revelation to me, introducing me as it did to his "harshly formed, powerful poems," as Randall Jarrell describes them, with "their tone of somewhat forbidding authority," several of which lodged in my memory—not only scenarios but also images and even phrases from "The Mediterranean," "Aeneas at Washington," "The Wolves," and "The Swimmers."

I had studied and fallen in love with John Crowe Ransom's poems in my first English course at the university, and there Tate's name had arisen in such a reverential way that when I came on the poster taped to the west entrance of my dormitory, announcing that "America's most distinguished man of letters" would receive the university's Award for Distinction in Literature and read from his work, I retrieved a suit (navy blue with a red-and-white windowpane) from home and became the only student suitably attired for the occasion. "Allen would have appreciated that," Peter Taylor later told me—my dressing up, that is; for Tate had been rather a dandy. My impression of the man himself had not gibed with Taylor's characterization, perhaps because Tate, with his "enormous brow," as Lowell depicts it, "cannonball head of a snowman," was skin and bones and his left sock, when he crossed his legs at the reception, drooped around a hairless, white ankle. I held out my program for him to sign, then crouched beside him and, wanting to connect with the man, asked how "Mr. Ransom" was. "Well," Tate said in a reedy smoker's voice, "John's eighty-five." I knew that, yes. "And he's revising his poems." At least he couldn't "expunge" them, Tate had told him, from the anthologies. "I can't help believing it's some senile compunction driving John to reject his early work."

Tate fished from the right side-pocket of his jacket a pack of Winstons, shook one out, and lit it, whereupon I switched from Kent 100s, the brand of that favorite professor who'd taught me Ransom, to Winston—as later, when MacLeish orders Scotch before his dinner of lamb chops at The Market Restaurant ("Famous for Food" and "featuring Maine lobsters and U.S. prime Western steaks"), I resolve that stomach Scotch I will and it will be Johnny Walker…"Red or Black," the waitress asks MacLeish: "Black," he says, and "You thought otherwise?" his tone implies. Of course I can't afford it. (Less unaffordable, the Dickeys' Scotch is Cutty Sark.)

"Poor devil," MacLeish continues in that letter. "I can't *bear* to think of the anguish he has to face." Tate is bedridden with emphysema and losing his sight to macular degeneration. "You used the phrase 'man of letters' when you introduced me. It belongs to *him*. He is the last real American 'man of letters.' A beautiful and, when objective, just and honorable mind—a beautiful instrument. The rest are scholars which is a grand thing to be but different." (Though Tate's reviews of MacLeish's early verse were encouraging and, on balance, admiring, his "critical vocabulary," in particular the words "success" and "failure" wielded imperiously, rankled MacLeish.) "I think of him constantly—and the months ahead. God I wish I could *do* something for him!"

Why, MacLeish wonders aloud (the silver medal, which I've presented him, hanging from a ribbon around his neck)—why are we students here listening to this old man whom we'll surely never see again? And he proceeds to draw an analogy between himself as the ancient Mariner and us as the Wedding Guest in Coleridge's famous ballad—an analogy that threads through his recitation of his poems while the question itself goes unanswered.

How deeply he'd have been willing to explore the analogy and how he'd have answered the question who can say for sure? Here's a guess. Late in the poem by Coleridge, as the Mariner concludes his account of the voyage and the doomed ship's return to port in England, where it sinks in the harbor, he tells the mesmerized Wedding Guest about his encounter with a Hermit, how he entreated this Hermit to "shrieve" him—to hear his confession and impose appropriate penance—whereupon the Hermit bluntly asked, "What manner of man art thou?" It was then, as Coleridge notes in the margin, that "the penance of life [fell] on him." That penance is, when comes a sudden pain, to tell his tale—a pain such as the Hermit's question caused. As the Mariner explains (lines 578–581),

> Forthwith this frame of mine was wrenched
> With a woeful agony,
> Which forced me to begin my tale;
> And then it left me free

—free, that is, from agony. While the Hermit asked about the Mariner as a particular man, MacLeish, I'm guessing, heard the question as a philosophical one about *man*: as MacLeish's sphinx puts it in "What Riddle Asked the Sphinx," a later poem, "What riddle is it has for answer, Man?" While the Mariner's tale accounts for himself, perhaps the *telling* of the tale—this effort to account—enacts a response to that ontological question about the human being. "Man is creature to whom meaning matters," MacLeish asserts in "The Infinite Reason," another later poem.

My guess is also that MacLeish understood the Mariner's "penance" to be a life lived through the telling of a tale whose inciting incident ("I shot the Albatross") expresses a mysterious, uniquely human, nihilistic willfulness—a life lived through the telling and *retelling* of that tale because the mystery of the psyche persists. In "Dr. Sigmund Freud Discovers the Sea Shell," MacLeish asks about the oceanic sound that issues from that shell, a symbol of the fathomless psyche, "what surf / Of what far sea upon what unknown ground / Troubles forever with that asking sound? / What surge is this whose question never ceases?" Life lived in such a way as responds to the question "What manner of man art thou?" is penance for being "man."

For MacLeish, not only the public recitation of his poems but also the making of them was his life sentence: "Man I am: poet must be," he affirms in "Reasons for Music," yet another later poem, and here he draws an analogy between his labor, the task of man-as-poet, and the activity of coral:

> Why do we labor at the poem?
> Out of the turbulence of the sea
> Flower by brittle flower, rises
> The coral reef that calms the water.

As the reef "calms the water" (although it does not *still* the surge of surf), the Mariner's tale, in the process of its telling, calms his turbulent psyche. Time and again, it frees him from the "woeful agony" aroused by the Hermit's question—does so by testifying to the conversion of that unfathomable, nihilistic willfulness to a love that imitates God's love of "man and bird and beast...All things both great and small" (lines 613–615) and thereby establishing order as only the "obdurate" human mind can do: "Tell me," the water asks the wind in the last of MacLeish's *Songs for Eve*, "what is man / That immortal order can?"

Fundamentally, that question about himself as man is as pertinent to the Wedding Guest as to the Mariner—and to us mesmerized students as to MacLeish, whose triumph is "the old man's triumph, to pursue / Impossibility"—the impossibility of accounting definitively for himself as man—"and take it, too." (Here I pull out of context lines from "'The Wild Old Wicked Man,'" a still later poem.)

Made of "solid silver," according to a note in the program, that medal which I hung around MacLeish's neck had been designed and cast by a sculptor in Camden. A non-traditional student at the university, Lewis T. Chapman had made a career in the Air Force and retired at the rank of colonel. Irregularly shaped—not at all a conventional round medallion—the medal bore on one side a bas-relief portrait of

100

MacLeish, as the previous year's medal did of Robert Lowell. "I look like Beethoven," Lowell mumbled. MacLeish remarked that he looked like Eisenhower. Engraved on the back there was "MacLeish" misspelled: "McLeish."

Some weeks after MacLeish's visit, the medal has been engraved anew or else recast—I don't know which—and so I drive with Ashley the forty minutes east from Columbia to historic Camden, historic because it was the site of the worst defeat of the Continental Army by the British, under Lord Cornwallis, in the Revolutionary War.

For lunch the Colonel recommends DeBruhl's Café, a typical small-town diner (which is still, forty years later, in business). At least one of us, Ashley or I, must have eaten fish: in the poem of mine that emerges from the occasion, "lunchtime's fishbone, splintered near / an eyetooth, had begun to throb." Anyway, there in the parking lot, as it troubles us to find, is a dead crow hanging by its feet from the rear bumper of a pick-up truck, its wings outspread.

In that poem, which Daryl Hine publishes in *Poetry* in 1976, I am trying out authorial stances if not also voices. The accentual measures I take from Yeats and Dickey; the central metaphor of original sin as a dark garment derives from a phrase, "the human fabric," of Robert Penn Warren's; another phrase, "grain-tinctured," which describes the dawn, I steal from *The Prelude*; and the stance I owe to Tate, whose poems I've been avidly reading, at least the ones in *The Norton Anthology of Modern Poetry*, where a footnote on the concluding lines of "Last Days of Alice" quotes Martin Luther's directive: "Sin boldly"—which delights me, growing up Lutheran.

To "sin boldly"—this is the speaker's implicit directive to "you" in "Outside DeBruhl's Café." For the speaker of the poem, the dead crow symbolizes the "certain dark" that opposes the order of things that daylight renders visible—or to put the opposition in a theological way, the nothingness that opposes being, which proceeds from God. Whoever has killed the crow and hung it upside down from the bumper has made a prideful display of self-righteousness, or so the speaker of the poem interprets his motive. At the sight of the crow you feel yourself to be in the grip of a darkness that only Christ, like a hound with the "terrible grace of his nails," can undo. The concluding lines of "Last Days of Alice" read in part: "O God of our flesh, return us to Your wrath, / Let us be evil could we enter in / Your grace"—lines that fairly well summarize my speaker's stance.

In another poem, "Winter Mask," Tate poses this question: "why it is man hates / His own salvation." Perhaps it is an obscure revulsion of being with God that impels the Mariner to shoot the albatross; perhaps it is his captivation by nothingness that the dead albatross then comes to symbolize when it hangs crucifix-like from the Mariner's neck. This is, in any case, what my poem's crow, upside down like Peter crucified, embodies. What "Outside DeBruhl's Café" owes to MacLeish, it owes to his Mariner.

Along with two other poems of mine, "Outside DeBruhl's Café" appears in an issue of *Poetry* that features early poems by Ezra Pound. If MacLeish reads *Poetry*, surely these will have caught his eye. Whether in fact they have—whether he's read *my* poems—I never know; nor do I know whether Dickey ever reads them. One of them, "Midnight Oil," pays such an obvious stylistic homage to Robert Lowell that I hesitate to show the poems to Dickey, who described Lowell as "My oldest friend [portentous pause] and rival" when Lowell accepted the invitation of us students to receive the university's Award for Distinction in Literature in 1974. Years later, when I do tell Dickey about the crow outside DeBruhl's Café, he relates an incident: when he was serving as poetry consultant at the Library of Congress and living in Leesburg, Virginia, he was driving home across Key Bridge and a seagull flashed in front of the car. Once home, he found it "crucified," lodged between the grill bars of that maroon, 1966 Corvette Stingray. He pondered a poem about it, but never came to write it.

"Crucified seagull. Shades of 'The Ancient Mariner,' one of his favorite poems," Dickey's son Christopher observes when I report the conversation. Surely Dickey also made the connection! When I quote to Chris that quiz of a stanza about the course of the ship as it relates to the sun, he responds, "For reasons that probably had to do with WWII and the real carnage he saw and imagined, the lines I think that most affected him were 'The many men so beautiful! / And they all dead did lie'" (lines 236–237). Now I am pondering the poem *as I conceive it* that Dickey never wrote—in which not a sailor but rather an Air Corps veteran and amateur archer crucifies by accident a seagull on the grill of his sports car, and this act, because it triggers the memory of the Mariner's "many men," indicts him for the deaths of those comrades-in-arms whom he survived: "The dead against the dead and on the silent ground / The silent slain," as MacLeish famously depicts the dead in France whom he survived.

Why is it that for forty years MacLeish has traveled with me? There is that haunting cadence, yes. There are some two dozen poems I love, maybe especially "Eleven," "'Not Marble Nor the Gilded Monuments,'" "You, Andrew Marvell," "Epistle to Be Left in the Earth," "Cook County," "Calypso's Island," "The Old Man to the Lizard," "What Riddle Asked the Sphinx," "Captivity of the Fly," "Rainbow at Evening."

There is also that couple, those two sweethearts whom MacLeish invited to have breakfast with him the morning of his flight home. In a letter two years later, right as Ashley and I were embarking on our Grand Tour, MacLeish wrote, "I can see you both at that table," and since he could, I see us there as well; and because, this morning after his reading, he's still to me the ancient Mariner and we are his mesmerized guests, I picture that breakfast—I ordered a western omelet and feel embarrassed by my extravagance when the bill arrives and he takes it for granted that he is treating us—I see it as a feast, a wedding feast of sorts, that binds us aspiring writers to a life of writing, which becomes a marriage of continuous critique-as-courtship as I make my poems and Ashley Mace Havird makes hers, her poetry and her fiction.

No doubt that invitation to breakfast was MacLeish's cordial way of ensuring that his ride got him to the airport with time to spare.

Forty years later, and for the first time since 1977, we're in Paris, Ashley and I; it's rained and now a diaphanous shimmer suffuses the air—we're on the Quai de Montebello, right about to cross the bridge, the Pont au Double, to Notre-Dame when we sight it, a rainbow, two rainbows in fact, the one above the other scarcely visible, spanning the quay and descending somewhere behind the cathedral...and I find myself reciting from memory:

Rainbow over evening, my
Iris of the after-sky,
show me, now the gales are by,
where the gold is.
When the rain
crazed the whirling weather vane
I never wondered. I knew then.
Gold was where the heart could find.

Now the heart is out of mind
in this late hour your seal has signed,
show me, *arc-en-ciel*, bright bow,
where the gold is hidden now.

A late poem, appearing in *"The Wild Old Wicked Man" and Other Poems* (1968), MacLeish's last book of all new poems, "Rainbow at Evening" is an old man's poem, depicting as it does the speaker at sundown after a lifetime's day of rain and wind from every quarter, depicting perhaps (impersonal though the poem is) the poet himself, MacLeish, whose mind was never quiet—"I cannot remember a quiet period in the life of my mind...It was either anguish at the sense of sin, or it was intellectual doubt, or it was...rage at [social] injustice"—who was taken by chance, after five years in Paris as a poet, to one career after another: to *Fortune* magazine as a journalist in 1929, to the Library of Congress as librarian in 1939, to the State Department as assistant secretary of state for cultural and public affairs in 1944, to Harvard University as Boylston Professor of Rhetoric and Oratory in 1949; who knew in his heart that a poet was "what I really wanted to be and was"; who found fame as he desired ("I suppose you start out...with that lust for fame to which Keats confessed and to which, I guess, we should all confess—all of us who practice an art, certainly") but who came in old age to "wonder on occasion why that poem," *Conquistador*, whose 1933 Pulitzer affirmed that the journalist at *Fortune* was a poet, "has slipped so completely out of sight"; who asks now that the "gales are by," "show me, *arc-en-ciel*, bright bow, / where the gold is hidden now"—*where indeed*, that off-rhyme seems to add.

"Your plans for France are exciting even at 85! I envy you," Mac-Leish wrote in April of 1977 before Ashley and I set out on our Grand Tour. Later, in September, he observed: "Paris has indeed changed since our day but the fundamental underlying city is still there in spite of the irrelevant and altogether ridiculous sky-scraper." No doubt Mac-Leish was referring contemptuously to the recently constructed (1969–1973) Tour Montparnasse, then the tallest skyscraper in France. As for the city that's still there, the building at 85, boulevard Saint-Michel "up opposite the École des Mines with the Luxembourg out in front" where MacLeish settled in 1923 with Ada, his wife, and their little boy, Kenneth, and infant daughter, Mimi, "in a cold-water flat on the fourth floor" is there, and in the stone wall of the École Nationale Supérieure des Mines de Paris, there are shell-holes from its bombardment during World War One, in January 1918, and during the liberation of Paris in August 1944; and there is the building at 44, rue du Bac where the MacLeishes rented a *pied-à-terre* in 1925 and which a plaque identifies as the house where André Malraux wrote *La Condition Humaine* (1933).

La Samaritaine, however, that enormous Art Deco department store on the Right Bank, near the eastern tip of the Ile de Cité, which opened on the site in 1900, closed for business in 2005. When Ashley and I were here in 1977 and the weather was, while not bone-numbing and wet as it had been in London, still chilly and damp and I was coming down with a cold, I had—yes, I was on a quest—to buy a beret, but not just any beret: one like MacLeish had worn, unselfconsciously, no matter his attire, sports coat or the three-piece suit he donned for the reading. (Dickey favored wide-brimmed hats, but while I'd coveted that black felt hat of his with "The Shadow" incised on the sweatband and even tried it on, I never could have sported it for real.) So there we were, Ashley and I, on which of La Samaritaine's eleven floors who can remember where there were bins of berets, as you won't find anywhere at all forty years later in Paris. But the sizes! There were two numbers stamped on the sweatband. As the elderly clerk explained, who spoke no English and chuckled whenever I spoke French, the first number gave the head-size, the other the "*plateau*"—he positioned his hands as best as he could around that part of the beret, the excess fabric, which folds. Mine had to be a snug beret—a peasant's beret was what Mac-Leish had worn and not a floppy artist's. The clerk rummaged the bins, even the drawers beneath the bins. Time and again he'd point: "*Pure laine*," pronouncing slowly the words on the label, "*imperméable.*"

A Note on Sources

My principal source for biographical information is Scott Donaldson, *Archibald MacLeish: An American Life* (Houghton Mifflin, 1992). In general, direct quotations from MacLeish on matters autobiographical come from Bernard A. Drabeck and Helen E. Ellis, eds., *Archibald MacLeish: Reflections* (U of Massachusetts P, 1986). See Drabeck and Ellis for MacLeish's description of the effect of his career in government on his life in poetry; also for MacLeish's description of the family's flat in Paris. (For "Accordimine," a transcription error, read "École des Mines," as I have done.) Quotations from MacLeish's letters, except the ones to me, derive from *Letters of Archibald MacLeish, 1907 to 1982*, ed. R. H. Winnick (Houghton Mifflin, 1983); quotations from MacLeish's poems from the posthumous *Collected Poems, 1917–1982* (Houghton Mifflin, 1985). The long sentence summarizing Mac-Leish's career, which follows the poem "Rainbow at Evening," pulls passages from several sources: "I cannot remember..." from William H. MacLeish, *Uphill with Archie: A Son's Journey* (Simon and Schuster, 2001); "what I really wanted..." from Drabeck and Ellis; "I suppose..." from Benjamin DeMott's *Paris Review* interview with Mac-Leish (issue 58, summer 1974); "has slipped so..." from Drabeck and Ellis.

FIVE

EARLY POEMS

MIDNIGHT OIL

After half-finishing Mollie Panter-Downes's
At the Pines: Swinburne and Watts-Dunton in Putney

The Winter Solstice swaddles me in sleep.
A starburst through my window rips the pall
Of midnight from my bedroom's sea-gray wall.
I'm drowning in the Galilean Lake.
Jehovah's fuming oarsmen cannot shake
The tide's death grip. Waves fork and flicker, leap.
The surface steams with venom, scalding me.
My eyes are running, melting from the heat.
Charon, your hand! This isn't Galilee.
I'm slipping, sliding under, and my feet
Find nothing there. I'm on the Hated Styx.
I clutch the pilot's hand. This can't be Hell;
His sweat embalms me with its fishy smell.
O nightmare, midnight oil! I cast away
The bedspread. On the wall, my crucifix,
The blear-eyed Corpus Christi carved in wood
Batting his shaggy lids against the light,
Which seems to singe them, for he squirms. This night—
A dumb show shadowing the Passion Play.
I twist with him, so prickly is my mood,
As if upon a splitting skull's white throne.
I summon Swinburne, for that pagan's hands
Assailed with thunderclaps Golgotha's god;
And now on Putney's balding slope he stands
To strike with lightning's eagle-headed rod
And detonate the Law-envenomed stone.
The pulpits trembled once; now you are old,
Your ballads mutter through a beard of mold,
Of waste and welter knells the wan North Sea.

O Proserpine, a virgin stokes the dark
That winters where you bloomed. As if insane
With moonlight, buried channels boil; my brain
Is waterlogged...until the dog, its bark
Exploding from three gullets, rouses me.

WASPS IN WINTER

On dry October's crust
leaves blown like spume
from waterfalls of oaks—
now only one thing bloomed
and it was rust.

A field day for the wasps that swarmed
outside the blinds
while crosswinds shook
the season's skeletal red brick.
One afternoon
two dozen of their army stormed
a broken fascia. That platoon
held rank until
the House & Garden spray
struck nerves—the unit lay
defiled upon a windowsill.
As autumn droned,
only a straggle of survivors
fluttered among the host
of slaughtered lovers.

Now winter grinds
the wasps, old lovers, past
vexations of
a morning-after's battlefield of love.
Stained bed sheets, pubic strands askew,
sloughed from the tangled web
of their geometry,
love's victims stricken in lust's after-dew—
all vanish to neutrality,
this season's attitude.

The crosswinds ebb.
Then like a paralyzing fungus, frost.
No insects in the rafters. Pilots steer
through other twilights, east
along this latitude.
Entranced, a virgin peers
from her rich bed of straw.
A year recycles the old law—
like thorns of rust,
wasps wreathe her infant's head.

OUTSIDE DEBRUHL'S CAFÉ

1.

When the human fabric snarls,
it dogs you as a toothache might.
Sometimes it scales your spine—
crisscrosses unravel in threads
of light on the black backdrop.
Shed what beasts endow you with,
the myth of a tailored tweed,
houndstooth or herringbone.
Be certain that is all
or you strip from the soul
what the Hound of Heaven pursues
with the terrible grace of its nails.
Be certain your eye for detail
misses no chance of light:
in chiaroscuro a grove
of midnight gathers the Son
where the primitive fish
splinters with hope like light.

2.

Once you beheld what the heart
holds in its color of caring,
solicitous certitude forever green
where what was certain was doubtless dark.
(Light and time discover perspective,
stark matrices of shifting oaks,
where night's a pine forest of clouds.)
No mathematic in that certain dark,
no geometric fantasy of stars,

classics of beasts, heroes, and gods
jealous of their universal squares.
Pine needles of steel from season's first freeze
traced that night's slate-like severity,
a fierceness to each depth of sound.

A shift in the forest's rank and file
splintered those mythologies;
a scraping honed the depth of light
when dawn's grain-tinctured glare beheld
the forest as a cube of dawn.
Pines and bordering staffs of oaks
rebuked with a crackling like laughter
a bladed army of grass
advancing in time. Where you stood
on that meadow's plane of dawn
an undertow swelled from the thaw
trouncing whole companies of grass.
Your wristwatch blazed with the absolute
ferocity of sun, to enthrall
amid feathers ruffling the dawn
the instinctive swoop of a crow
to possess in its personal
darkness what totally shone.

3.

Noontime had gilt that neck of the woods,
strewn autumn on the graveled drive,
gold-leafed as a freeway to Heaven.
But lunchtime's fishbone, splintered near
an eyetooth, had begun to throb.
Outside DeBruhl's Café
the crow whose flight had leveled dawn
dangled in a change of light,
suspended from a beam of chrome,

the bumper of a Chevrolet,
spread-eagled in a downward curve,
almost absurd, a mangy thing of death—

or Euclid drawn and quartered on
a schoolchild's dog-eared plane,
or the vagrant Apostle gaffed on white
pine splintered by nails of light:
the knowledge that what was certain
in the dark was your certain need;
and your greatcoat gathered you
into its beastly tweed.

THE SNOW

...falling faintly through the universe—James Joyce

Within the sea-reared coil
The gaze is fixed, eye numb.
Sharp tongues, descanting, roil
The ear—the Sirens hum.

Far southward their career
Has yet to agitate
The lazy atmosphere.
My syllables vibrate

Not even with profane
Surfside-defiling gulls,
Which cruise in the inane
Above a faint sea's pulse.

Fair winds cast clouds adrift,
Salt winds that blear and curl
In coves. If waves do lift,
They crawl, collapse, and swirl.

By lantern-light the strand
Is sandbagged. Hordes of waves
Wheel headlong toward the land.
The North Atlantic raves.

The eye, though glazed, dilates.
Ear-ringing salvos rout
The gulls that ply the straits.
The stricken stars fall out,

And reeling from the blind
On trails they blaze with light,
Beyond themselves they wind,
Hurled from that whirling height.

Here now the starlight, flake
By flake, is sifting. Neap
Tides shiver, whitecaps wake;
As if from caves of sleep

Winds tumble, seagulls weave.
When broad swells steepen, splash
The reefs and spill, the heave
Of distance seems to crash.

IN THE WHITE ROOM

Infertility

Spaced a month apart,
which her mania counts as a minute,
from floor to ceiling, doors.
Toe-tagged, the bodies of victims
keep stiff-leggedly cool
on slabs behind such doors
as these that checker four
snowblindingly stainless steel walls.

The white-out dizzies a woman,
who feels now with scattering palms
for handles to yank open doors
to vaults that vacantly yawn.
Where, in these catacombs, do
her quickening children hunch?

Her time is running out
of months: a minute hand hurtles—
it spears them, she winces, they rupture.
The clock, announcing the month,
strikes them off one a minute.

Meanwhile the snow-crust hums
with currents that tingle her feet.
Her moist palm grazes a handle,
which grips her hand in a flash.
The minute hand sizzles, it splinters,
it gnarls into roots in her belly.
A ravishing surge of it forks
into branches that flex into leaf.

Her limbs, irrigated by veins
of lightning, stagger with shade,
with new generations of green,
above a turned field in a delta.

The door to a vault has banged open,
a vault where there huddles no child.
Its absence, an eye-scouring yawn,
bleaches the plow-land, the tree
spirals—a funnel of dust.

Amid this grainy dissolve,
this sandblasted landscape of grief,
a wasp-waisted figure of time
is exhausting herself in a dance
to deliver one infant at least
who fills out the flimsy, pale skin
of the ghost that she monthly conceives.

DOWNRIVER WITH UNCLE PAUL

Now Winter plants its pickax. Underground
a starburst of deep freeze, and Uncle Paul
clod-cold. I curl in bed

and try to go to sleep. My wristwatch hums,
the wristwatch newly mine;
for Uncle Paul, at fifty-nine, is dead.

The Accutron, its luminous green face
emblazoned with a trademark tuning fork,
hums as with light. The dresser top,
that drumhead, amplifies the sound
until the whole dark bedroom glows
behind my shut eyelids an eerie green.
I huddle as within his humming star.

Another sound
augmenting, then diminishing that tone—
outside the house a hum that comes and goes.
Believe in God, and it won't have to come
from any mere transformer; for tonight
sounds carry an eternity. I make

believe it emanates
from God's own tuning fork. Try as it might
to keep the music of the spheres on pitch,
it cannot now; for Uncle Paul,
game-legged Uncle Paul has, lurching, come.

She'd watched him walk across the living room
and fall, Grandmother told me once—

a growing boy whom infantile
paralysis had spilled. My father's baby brother.

Summers I'd spend a week or so with her,
and weekends he'd show up to ride
his horses, motorcycles…Bored
on one occasion with his toys, he bought
himself a boat. His plan: we'd motor down
the Saluda River to Lake Murray,
eat catfish at Holiday Shores,
and be back home by dark.

Well, homeward every cove
looked like the river's mouth
until we ventured in and failed to find
the snags that choked it. Night
thickened. The small prop churned the lake
not much. The outboard knocked
against the muffling whine
of midges, while my flashlight bent its beam
to sweep aside the dense bug-haze. At last
the river shut its mouth on us,
and we became the river's word unsaid.

My uncle cut the engine. Anchorless
but caged within unnavigable snags—
from somewhere he fished out a mason jar
of corn, white lightning, killed it, then
pitched over onto seats laid flat for a bed.

Such an eruption then of snores I looked
for that black river, like a dragon's tongue,
to foam with lava. Sparks
or else the gibes of gadflies burned
my ears, elsewhere raised welts,

and less and less I seemed the weightless soul
a body floating feels itself to be
and ever more a beast, the weight
of whose own bitten corpse its burden is.

Meanwhile my uncle's brand new Accutron
was humming its one reconciling note....

God hurls his bolt, a father to his child:
Now go to sleep. But Uncle Paul,
who had a thing for watches, hums
a luminous green song of time.

A night of utter cold, a night of sounds
that carry an eternity—tonight
a body ought to rise
upon a call of light, a breath
that quivers with one's secret given name.

But I, sleep's orphan, huddle now
within the drone of gravity itself,
the gravity of a collapsing star
that tugs its neighbors from their certain rounds,
that hum which tunes the orchestra of stars
to its off key.